A Scottish Migration to Alexandria

# A Scottish Migration to Alexandria

By Ellen J. Hamilton

**YLW DOT**

A Scottish Migration to Alexandria
Library of Congress Control Number:
2021917335

ISBN 978-0-9763725-1-6

Produced in Alexandria, Virginia
Manufactured in the United States of America

Book design, photography and illustration by Ellen Hamilton
except where noted
Edited by Vera A. Pastore, Word Choreography

**YLW DOT**

Yellow Dot Publishing
Alexandria, VA 22301
yellowdotpublishing.com

"The history of humans
is a history of migration."

— Anonymous

# Contents

# Acknowledgments

For this most exciting project of my life, I have many people to be thankful for. This endeavor would not have been possible without my loving husband, Andrew Hamilton, for being supportive throughout, for his patience and honest critique.

It all began when Shona Ferguson from near Erskine, Scotland, gave me the book by Derek Alexander, *Renfrewshire, A Scottish County's Hidden Past.* I was pleased to contact Mr. Alexander, and I am grateful for the on-camera interview that he gave me at Newark Castle in Port Glasgow, Scotland. I had the good fortune of contacting a former British Member of the House of Lords, James Erskine, Earl of Mar and Kellie. I was interested in his family's original ownership of parts of Renfrewshire, including his namesake town of Erskine. His ancestors built the stately home, Erskine House, now called Mar Hall. It is an elegant hotel overlooking the Clyde River which serves a nice high tea, and is worth a visit. The Earl graciously gave me an extensive telephone interview.

In Alexandria I am grateful to J. Lance Mallamo, former director of the Office of Historic Alexandria, for making me aware of William Gregory through his "Out of the Attic" articles in the *Alexandria Times* newspaper. Thank you to Lance for giving me my first interview, and to Nicole Quinn for facilitating. Michael Lee Pope, Alexandria historian and author, has been helpful with information, and a great on-camera interview on a cold January morning at Alexandria's historic Carlyle House. The interview was facilitated by Susan Hellman, former manager at Carlyle House Historic Park.

My invaluable sources in Kilmarnock, Scotland, were first of all, Frank Spence, who is an expert on the Gregory Family. Frank and I agreed that we are the only two people in the world who know this much about the Gregorys! That may be about to change with the publication of this book. Also in Kilmarnock, I had great help from Jason Sutcliffe from Kilmarnock's grand museum, the Dick Institute. Mr. Sutcliffe showed me Gregory family documents, exhibits on weaving, and the actual piano that was played by Eliza Gregory for poet Robert Burns. Thank you to Fraser Wilson at the *Kilmarnock Standard*, who took down my story as I was leaving town, and wrote an article that was published the next day.

With the help of Dr. Donald C. Dahmann, historian of the Old Presbyterian Meeting House, and the many resources that he provided me with, I was able to miraculously find descendants of William Gregory. The first descendant I contacted was Philip "Pete" Gibson, who has been helpful since our first, rather surprised, telephone conversation. Other Gregory descendants, Martica Gibson, Gregory Gibson, and Karen Shaw, shared documents and images from the family with me. Great big thanks to Margaret Kennedy of Old Town Productions for teaching me about video production, guiding my video interviews, reading my manuscripts, and tutoring us for voice-over work.

I want to thank retired archaeologist Barbara Magid, Office of Historic Alexandria; Eleanor Breen, Alexandria City Archaeologist; Daniel Lee, historian at the Office of Historic Alexandria; Gretchen Bulova, director of the Office of Historic Alexandria; Jay Roberts for his *Jaybird's Jottings*; Larry Moffi of Settlement House Books; Alexandria historian Edward "Ted" Pulliam; D. David Heiby, Cemetery Superintendent at Old Presbyterian Meeting House; my cousin Elmer J. Halley, Jr., retired U.S. Navy Captain; Stephen Halperson of Tisara Photography, for use of his studio; Todd Healy for the use of his hand-colored Alexandria prints; Lynn Fallowfield for the fundraiser tea and her Scottish accent for the voice-over; and Gail Hamilton for her performance of the Robert Burns poem.

In Scotland, many thanks to Scott Johnson and Guy Thompson of Mallard Productions in Glasgow; and Rob Ferguson at Dalgarven Mills in Kilwinning, Scotland, for letting me get great footage of his mill's refurbished water wheel in action. Thanks also to Heather Tetley of the Tetley Workshop in England for sending me images of early Scottish carpets.

In Greenock, Scotland, I had great help from Sandra Wilson at Watt Library. Ms. Wilson gave me a great walking tour from the Library to the Greenock Ocean Terminal, a deep water port for large cruise liners and cargo ships. There I met Hugh Hardie, Operations Manager, who showed me historic photos of the port. Thank you to Joe Gurney, historian, and Eric Webster at Greenock Central Library, who allowed an extemporaneous video interview about Greenock's history of Princes Pier.

I am grateful for help from librarians and staff of these libraries and museums:

Kate Waller Barrett Branch Library, Local History Special Collection, Alexandria, Virginia
Smithsonian Institution, Washington, DC
Mariners Museum, Newport News, VA
USS Constellation, Historic Ships of Baltimore
Paisley Heritage Museum, Paisley, Scotland
Mitchell Library, Glasgow, Scotland
Watt Library, Greenock, Scotland
Burns Monument Centre, Kilmarnock, Scotland
Dick Institute, Kilmarnock, Scotland
Mallaig Heritage Centre, Mallaig, Scotland
National Museum of Scotland, Edinburgh, Scotland

During the earlier filmmaking part of this project, I was always holding a fundraiser. Many thanks to these donors: Steven Halperson, Ann Rosser, Nora and Cliff Johnson, Ray and Bob Hamilton, Robyne and Stuart Hamilton, Holly Bloom, Dan J. Alpert, Karen Day, Cynthia Hurrle, Amanda Socci, Deborah Nolan, Elaine Flynn, Ellyn Ferguson, Gay Stikeleather, Carl and Janine Rauscher, Pamela Mackenzie, Joe Bordonaro, Priscilla Brailsford, Virginia Burke, Dave and Caroline Emmerson, Julie Halperson, Meg MacDonald, Bill Newbrough, Jeff Peterson, Ted Pulliam, Bruce and Shannon Russell, Nina Tisara, Shira and Rusty Eller, Margaret and Buzz Rettig, Marcia Pickard, Dennis Reeder, Lon Jones, Barbara McFarland Hannover, Michael Howery, Daniel Gillis, Dan Simonds, Laura Jackson, Karen and Bill Kelly, Colin McDonald, Earl Hamilton, Karen Shaw, Jay Roberts, and Micah Wilkie.

Finally, my sincerest thanks to my parents, Clifford and Nora Johnson, for their examples set, boundless enthusiasm and encouragement, and always being willing to read my writings. I am ever so grateful to everyone mentioned and many more, who sent me things, answered my calls, returned my emails, and gave me their time and attention. Thank you all so much.

Kilmarnock town center, Kilmarnock Cross in the 1800s with the James Shaw statue, which was later replaced with a statue of Robert Burns and his publisher John Wilson.

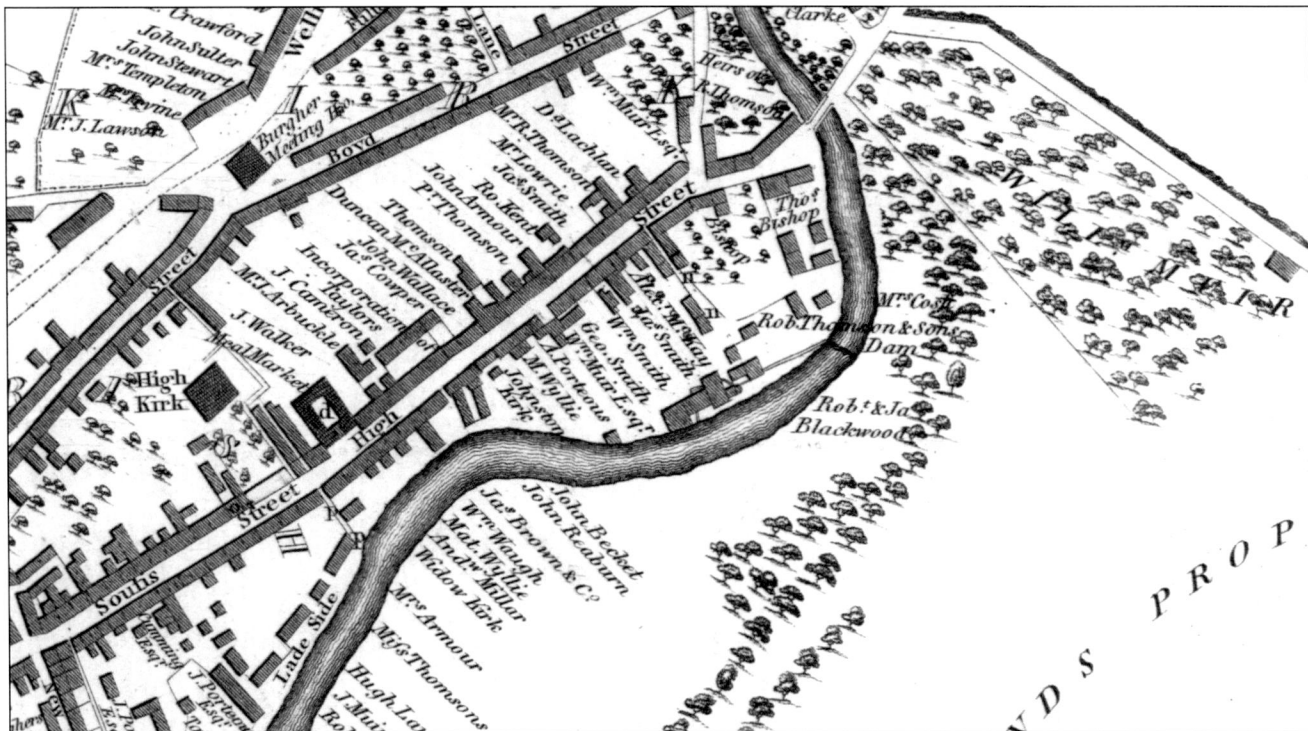

Plan of the Town of Kilmarnock, Surveyed by John Wood, 1819
Notice Rob. Thomson & Sons dam in the river, and the mill stream which appears to direct water to a cluster of buildings. This may have been a cotton weaving factory powered by water. Today there are no buildings by the river. It is a park, and it is hard to see where the mill stream had been. There are concrete remnants on the banks of the river and in the water. The High Kirk [Church] on the left is a funeral parlor today. Gregory family grave stones are at the southwestern corner of the church, flat on the ground.

Kilmarnock town center, Kilmarnock Cross, September 2021 with the Robert Burns and John Wilson statue. Photo by Frank Spence.

# Preface

On my first visit to Scotland, I wanted to head straight to the Highlands. People I spoke to about traveling there said they wanted to see the Highlands too. So much has been written about "The Clearances," the forced eviction and migration of Highland farmers. As I traveled to Scotland more often, I realized that because of the sheer number of people who live in the Lowlands, there must be a huge amount of human history there.

The Lowland region, or Central Belt, especially in the west is industrial. Not all areas are beautiful and some places suffer from local disdain for being rundown. Lately there has been a concerted effort to clean up, renovate and appreciate southern Scottish cities. Renfrewshire, the county in the southwest, just south of Glasgow, is where the Lowlands begin. This area is on the southern bank of the Clyde River. Just across the Clyde to the north and a few miles up lies the famous Loch Lomond. The Highlands stretch to the north from there.

I wondered whether most Scottish immigrants who ended up in America came from this Lowland region—the counties of Renfrewshire, Ayrshire, and Lanarkshire. These were industrial counties with many towns, rivers, and shuttered factories. I embarked on a great research project to see if most immigrants did indeed travel from the Lowlands. I wanted to know which ports people left from, when they left, and whether there were waves of migration.

A friend who knew I was interested in history and archaeology gave me the book, *Renfrewshire: A Scottish County's Hidden Past*, written by Scottish archaeologist Derek Alexander and the late Gordon McCrae. After a year of poring over that book, I suddenly had a sense of

11

the history all coming together for me. I could see the arc of human development, beginning with the early building of fledgling industry from wooden water wheels, harnessing power from the rivers that flow north to the Clyde. I could see how this resulted in the Cotton Revolution, modernization from a feudal system to the first widespread use of money, the building of towns for the first time, and a huge and sudden population explosion forcing people to travel in search of building materials that did not exist in Scotland to any great extent—specifically, wood.

I needed a main character whose story I could focus on. During my research I read an article in my local newspaper, the *Alexandria Times*, about a man from the Scottish town of Kilmarnock who had bought and expanded a house in Alexandria at 329 North Washington Street. Well, I had read all about Kilmarnock, it being a Lowland town involved in the Scottish textile industry. So I decided that William Gregory III (1789-1875) from Kilmarnock, Scotland, would be my man. Kilmarnock would be the beginning of the journey and Alexandria, Virginia, would be the destination. Thus ensued years of tracking down William's relatives, striking up contacts with historians, and visiting Kilmarnock.

Along the way I realized that my own ancestors came from Scotland. My middle name is McCaskill but for some reason our Scottish past had never been mentioned in my family. My parents were young and were more focused on child-rearing than on ancestry. When my grandmother passed away, I ended up being the one to go through all the old family photos. There I found a miniature painting of a woman in a plaid sash. It didn't say who she was, but it was speculated that it might have been a tourist painting of Flora MacDonald. I found that my family's McQueen side had lived in Greenock, Scotland. Greenock has always been a major port on the Clyde River and the place where so many Scots climbed aboard a ship, never to return. The McQueens are a Highland clan, so they must have been part of the many who had migrated south for work, when the clan system unraveled.

I contacted a museum in Kilmarnock, Scotland, looking for information on the Gregory family. I was directed to the Burns Monument Centre, who directed me to Frank Spence, a local Kilmarnock history buff. He would spend time at the Burns Monument Centre with an interest in William Gregory's brother, James Gregory, who became a prominent citizen in Kilmarnock. Frank sent me a steady stream of invaluable information on the Gregory family. A year or two later when I visited the town, I met Frank in person and he gave me a great tour of the High Church, the river, and other Gregory family sites.

As luck would have it, in the 1960s, a woman named Eileen Bennett found a trove of handwritten letters belonging to the Gregory family, tucked away in an old fish basket in a shop in England. She typed the letters and sent them to descendants of the Gregory family. Many of the letters, never before published, appear in this book.

All along, as I worked on this project, I intended it to be a film. I became involved with local film groups and learned a great deal. But finding major funding for a first-time filmmaker seems to be the place where most aspirational films go to die. After letting this project sit for more than a year and pondering options and a better ending, I got the inspiration to simply do what I could. I grew up with writers on both sides of my family, and writing being discussed at the dinner table. So write, I would.

Since this project was meant to be a film, I realize now that although it was great to do live interviews and get content on video, it meant I was focused more on the medium than the message. As a painter spends years honing their craft, and the writer learns the ins and outs of writing, once they sit down at that computer or canvas, the vast whiteness stares them down, and they realize they don't have a thing to say. So I told myself, forget about the film crew, the software, the paintbrush size. I need to sit down and write this story! As the Scottish poet Rabbie Burns wrote, "The best laid schemes of mice and men gang aft agley!" The best plans can often go wrong! In my case I should start with the story.

In my first writing of this as a film script, I stripped out anything I deemed unnecessary. So many fascinating side trips down the paths of related topics were cut. In the re-writing as a book, all the stories could be added back in.

This topic, the history of Scots migrating to America, is not one that is widely known. My grandfather was a Presbyterian minister in Alexandria and yet it was never mentioned that Presbyterianism came from Scotland. I have heard all my life that my family is "Scotch Irish." Again and again during this project people have told me they think they are Scotch Irish, although they only have a vague idea of what that means. I have often been asked how my "Ireland" project is coming along! Scotland is not on the mental map of Americans. This is not surprising, given the confusing nature of Britain's identity. When I met my Scottish husband, he explained to me the difference between "England" and "Britain." This difference gets confused quite a lot, even by educated people.

My hope is that this book will contribute to Americans' general knowledge of Scotland, the enormous scope of migration of people from Scotland to the United States, and why and how it happened.

Ellen Hamilton
Alexandria, Virginia 2021

A functional water wheel at The Dalgarven Mills in Kilwinning, Scotland

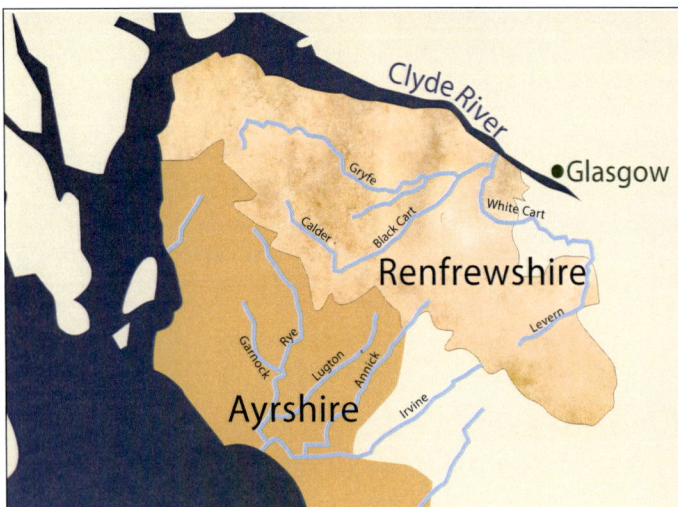

# Introduction

The southern part of Scotland has thousands of years of human history. Stone circles were built around the British Isles five thousand years before Christ. At that time people lived in small clans in hill forts, called *duns* in Gaelic. Many Scottish towns and families have names that contain *Dun* or the related *Dum* like Dumbarton (Fort of the Britons), Dunbar, Dunvegan, and Dumfries. About eighty years after the death of Christ, the Romans (people we know today as Italians), traveled north with their troops and held defensive forts on the hilltops along the Clyde River in an attempt to control the local tribes. They held these forts on and off for several hundred years. There are still markings in the land that show where the Roman forts were, and if you look closely, you might find Roman stone remnants in buildings nearby. This story of Scottish migration begins hundreds of years later, in the 1700s.

# The Lowlands and Scottish Descent

The Lowlands of Scotland are also called the Central Belt. *Low* does not mean southern. It means low lying. This land is where glaciers carved out two river valleys during the ice age. In the west the Clyde River flows past Scotland's largest city, Glasgow and out to the Atlantic Ocean. In the east the Forth River carves out a deep *firth* or estuary, and flows past Scotland's capital, Edinburgh, to the North Sea. It is no accident that Scotland's two largest cities, Glasgow and Edinburgh lie along this valley.

Americans generally have a romanticized notion of Scotland. Many like to think their Scottish ancestors came from the Scottish Highlands, an area that has been written about so often. But that is a false assumption; most of them came from the Lowlands. Many Americans say their ancestors are from Scotland but few can say where in Scotland, and even more rarely do people know which ship their family sailed over on, where it sailed from, or where it landed. It seems that our ancestors were so busy getting here and starting new lives, that they forgot to record these details for future generations.

The Lowlands of Scotland have always been far more populated than the Highlands. Millions of people have left the Scottish Lowlands over many years, including one man named William Gregory III. Eighteen-year-old William sailed from the Clyde River at one o'clock in the morning when the wind finally picked up, out past the Isle of Arran, past Ireland, and westward onto the Atlantic Ocean. He was on his way to America. It was March of 1807.

〰️

South of the Clyde River and the city of Glasgow lies the western county of Renfrewshire, and south of it is Ayrshire. These counties are some of the most industrial in Scotland and are

Using a wooden Runrig to plow the land

These photos were taken by Mary Ethel Muir Donaldson in the early 1900s in the Highlands of Scotland. They show us what life may have looked like in the Lowlands in the 1700s.

Water wheel mechanism

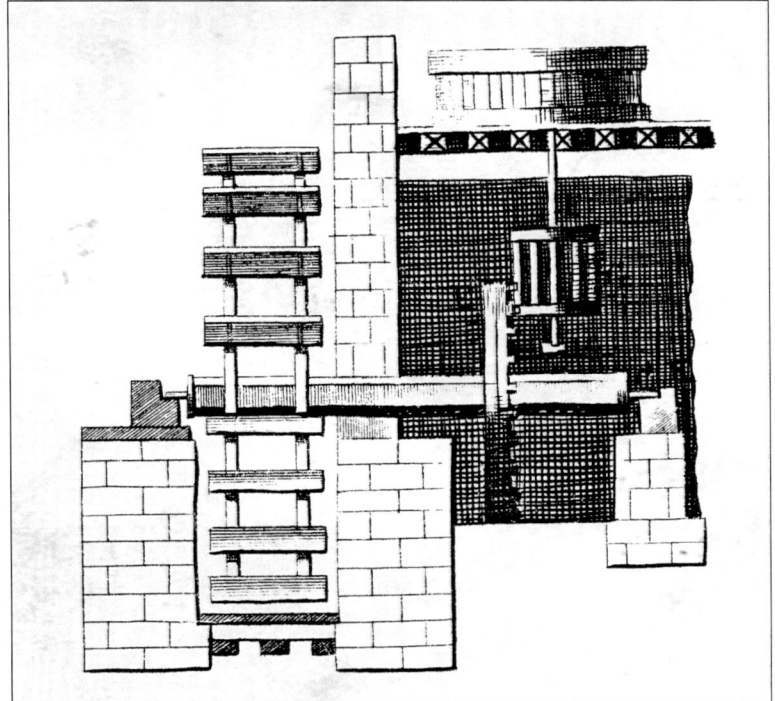

Digging peat for heating and cooking

part of Scotland's most populous region. The history of human development and modernization happened right here. It happened here because of the many rivers.

Scotland is famous for its frequent rain, drizzle, or *smirr* as the Scots call it. Regular rainfall is the reason for the many rivers that flow north into the Clyde through Renfrewshire. The Calder, the Black Cart, the White Cart, and the River Gryfe run north in an arc to the Clyde River from a series of gentle hills that run along the south of Renfrewshire County. This area was great for people to settle on the hilltops in fortified *duns* where they could keep an eye on threats.

In the 1100s the Church played a huge role in Scotland. Monks lived in fortified settlements by rivers where they built their monasteries, abbeys, and buildings. They had their own bakeries, gardens, and everything they needed to survive. One such settlement was along the White Cart River. The Abby still stands proudly at the center of Renfrewshire's largest city, Paisley. If you are traveling to Scotland by air, you might land in Paisley, at Glasgow Airport. These monks knew they could harness the power of the river to run a wheel, which could cause a spindle to turn, and thereby power all sorts of useful functions like grinding wheat. These wheels brought water power to Scotland. Rivers were the source of power for the first Scottish industries.

# A Primitive Life

Up until 1707, most Scots were farmers. Ninety percent of the Scottish population lived in the countryside. A few families would live in a cluster of houses called a farmtown (pronounced *fairm-toon*). Generations of families plowed the same small plot of land, using crude wooden plows called runrigs. Their land owner, or *laird*, had been granted that land by the King. Families were allowed to farm the land. The men were expected to serve as soldiers for the laird, to fight off threats from the neighbors. Rent was paid by giving a portion of the crops to the laird each season. But, over time, the soil in the family plot was getting worse. Crops were harder to grow. Sometimes there wasn't enough food.

In Scotland in the 1700s, there were just a few roads, connecting only larger towns. Muddy, overgrown paths lead from one family farmtown to another. No central government existed to clear roads. Scrubby common land surrounded the farmtowns, where families could gather wood, berries, and peat. In fact, people lived off this peat, which was basically dirt filled with ancient roots and plant matter. Trees were long since gone, so peat became the only heating fuel. People would dig up the peat in blocks and lay it out to dry. No wonder Scots were called "sons of dirt and mire" by their most famous poet, Robert Burns. The famous English writer Samuel Johnson wrote about the treeless region he witnessed from Scotland's southern border to one hundred miles north, while traveling through Scotland in 1773:

From the bank of the Tweed to St. Andrews I have never seen a single tree, which

Photos by
Mary Ethel Muir
Donaldson

Thatched cottage made
from local stone, with
a barefoot girl and a
woman outside.

Houston House in
Houston, Renfrewshire
goes back to the 1200s.
It has been owned by
various aristocratic owners
and has changed a lot over
the years. Today it houses
condos.

Photo by
Ellen Hamilton

I did not believe to have grown up far within the present century... The variety of sun and shade is here utterly unknown. There is no tree for either shelter or timber. The oak and the thorn is equally a stranger, and the whole country is extended in uniform nakedness.

In a naked country, small children ran naked. The trash was kept in a pile, called a *midden heap* in front of the house. The highlight of the week was church—the Presbyterian Church. That's where you would see your neighbors and get caught up on the news. You saw your landowner. He sat up in front, while you sat on a stool that you brought. There were no pews.

In Lowland Scotland, dukes, lords and earls owned castles, palaces and land. These lairds had been collecting rent from people for hundreds of years. Rent was called fee, or *feu*. The system was called *feudal*.

Barefoot boy in a kilt, holding fish

A woman knitting as she walks

Engraving of Robert Burns
Poet from Ayrshire, Scotland
1759-1796

John Erskine, 6th Earl of Mar, 1672-1732 and his
son Thomas, Lord Erskine, by Sir Godfrey Kneller.
Courtesy James Erskine, Earl of Mar and Kellie

# A Robert Burns Connection

Scotland's most famous poet is Robert Burns. Rabbie Burns was born in 1759 into a farming family in Ayrshire County. Farming was not Rabbie's favorite thing. He preferred writing love poems to his sweetheart. Though widely known for his poems about haggis, mice, and love, Rabbie's real interest was thorny political issues like the terrible social inequity in Scotland, and similar issues in France with the French Revolution, all of which made him quite controversial at the time. In the late 1700s, he wrote scathing poems about social injustices committed by the wealthy. Here is a poem, set up as the Devil speaking to landowners, that lays out the grievance of the Scottish landless farmers against the aristocratic, entitled land owners:

# Address of Beelzebub

By Robert Burns

Long life, my lord, and health be yours,
Unharmed by hungered Highland boors!
Lord grant no ragged, desperate beggar,
With dirk, sword, or rusty trigger,
May rob old Scotland of a life
She likes - as lambkins like a knife!

Faith! you and Applecross were right
To keep the Highland hounds in sight!
I doubt not! they would offer no better
Than let them once out over the water!
Then up among these lakes and seas,
They will make what rules and laws they please:
Some daring Hancock, or a Franklin,
May set their Highland blood to rankle;
Some Washington again may head them,
Or some Montgomerie, fearless, lead them;
Till (God knows what may be effected
When by such heads and hearts directed)
Poor dunghill sons of dirt and mire
May to Patrician rights aspire!
No sage North now, nor sager Sackville,
To watch and premier over the pack vile!
And where will you get Howes and Clintons
To bring them to a right repentance?
To cower the rebel generation,
And save the honor of the nation?
They, and be damned! what right have they
To meat or sleep or light of day,
Far less to riches, power, or freedom,
But what your lordship likes to give them?

But hear, my Lord! Glengary, hear!
Your hand's too light on them, I fear:

Your factors, grieves, trustees, and bailiffs,
I can not say but they do gaily:
They lay aside all tender mercies,
And strip the slovens to the bristles.
Yet while they are only distrained and robbed,
They will keep their stubborn Highland spirit.
But smash them! crush them all to chips,
And rot the bankrupts in the jails!
The young dogs, chastise them to the labour:
Let work and hunger make them sober!
The young girls, if they are at all good looking,
Let them in Drury Lane be lessoned!
And if the wives and dirty brats
Come begging at your doors and gates,
Flapping with rags and grey with vermin,
Frightening away your ducks and geese,
Get out a horsewhip or a bull dog,
The longest thong, the fiercest growler,
And make the tattered gypsies pack
With all their bastards on their back!
Go on, my Lord! I long to meet you,
And in my 'house at home' to greet you.
With common lords you shall not mingle:
The inmost corner beside the fireside,
At my right hand assigned your seat
Between Herod's hip and Polycrate,
Or (if you on your station weary)
Between Almagro and Pizarro,
A seat, I am sure you are well deserving of it;
And until you come - your humble servant,
Beelzebub
Hell

Robert Burns was born, and died in this cottage in Alloway, Ayrshire.

The room where Robert Burns died

Burns became successful with his poetry when his works were published in Kilmarnock, near his place of birth. The building where his books were printed was right on Kilmarnock's town square, and has since been demolished. Burns ended up living in the town of Dumfries, which is in a county south of Ayrshire.

The family of William Gregory III met Rabbie Burns on several occasions, including when a mutual friend hosted a party for Burns while he was passing through Kilmarnock. The Gregorys were a musically inclined family, so William's mother, Eliza Gregory, entertained the company by playing a song on her piano, the only piano in Kilmarnock at that time. Burns loved the song she played, "The Lass of Locherby." On a later visit, Burns again requested that song to be played. Today the Gregory family piano can be seen on display at Kilmarnock's museum called the Dick Institute.

Burns suffered a lifetime with periods of ill health and emotional outbursts. At the time of his early death at the age of 37, leaving a wife and three surviving children, Burns had alienated many of his best friends with his freely expressed sympathy with the French who were also battling aristocratic oppression with their French Revolution. He was buried without much fanfare in St. Michael's churchyard in Dumfries. Later, people realized he was the most important poet Scotland ever had, so they gave him a proper burial and moved him to his final and present location, the Burns Mausoleum at St. Michael's, twenty-one years after his death.

## The Gregory Family in Kilmarnock

The town of Kilmarnock (pronounced *Kill-mar-nuck*) is in Ayrshire County in the Scottish Lowlands. It was built along the western edge of a not too wide, not too deep river called Kilmarnock Water. The land on the eastern edge of the river rises up to form a steep, wooded ravine. The western side is reasonably flat, so the main road crosses over the river on the northern edge of town, right where the river curves to the south. You can stand on that little bridge and peer down into the dark, shady water below. Main Street runs parallel to Kilmarnock Water, and between the road and the river there is just enough land to build some dwellings with a bit of yard behind. People moved into Kilmarnock from the countryside and settled on that piece of land along Main Street. The town's aristocratic family—the Boyds—were lords of Kilmarnock for over four hundred years. Their stone castle lies about a mile north of the bridge.

During the 1700s, Kilmarnock's population grew. One of the first families to settle there was the family of merchant William Gregory I, whose grandson is the topic of this book. The land next to the bridge, where the river curves to the south, belonged to the Thomsons. To harness the power of the shallow river, a dam would be needed, so a dam was built across the river to guide water into a mill stream. A water wheel turned, creating power. A carpet weaving company was

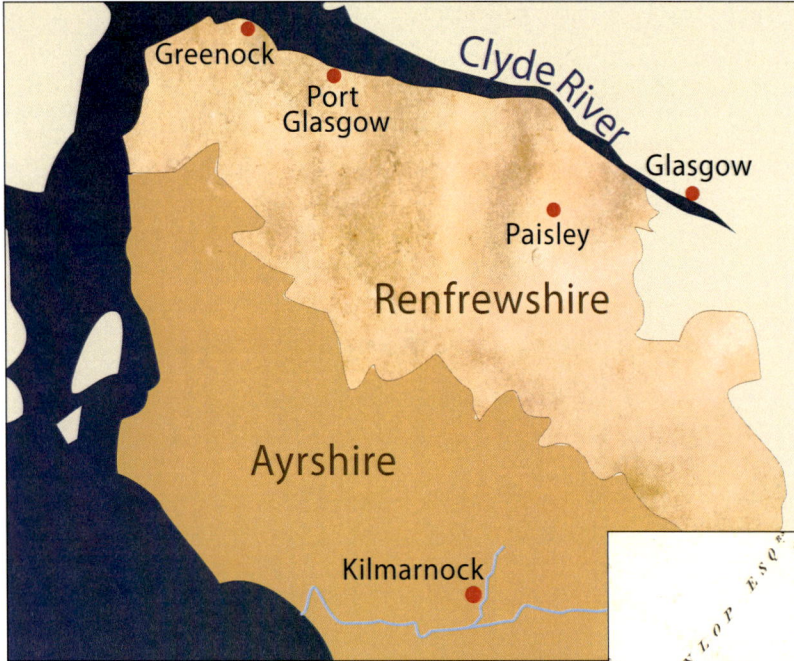

King George III on a guinea piece

William Gregory II, courtesy of Karen Shaw

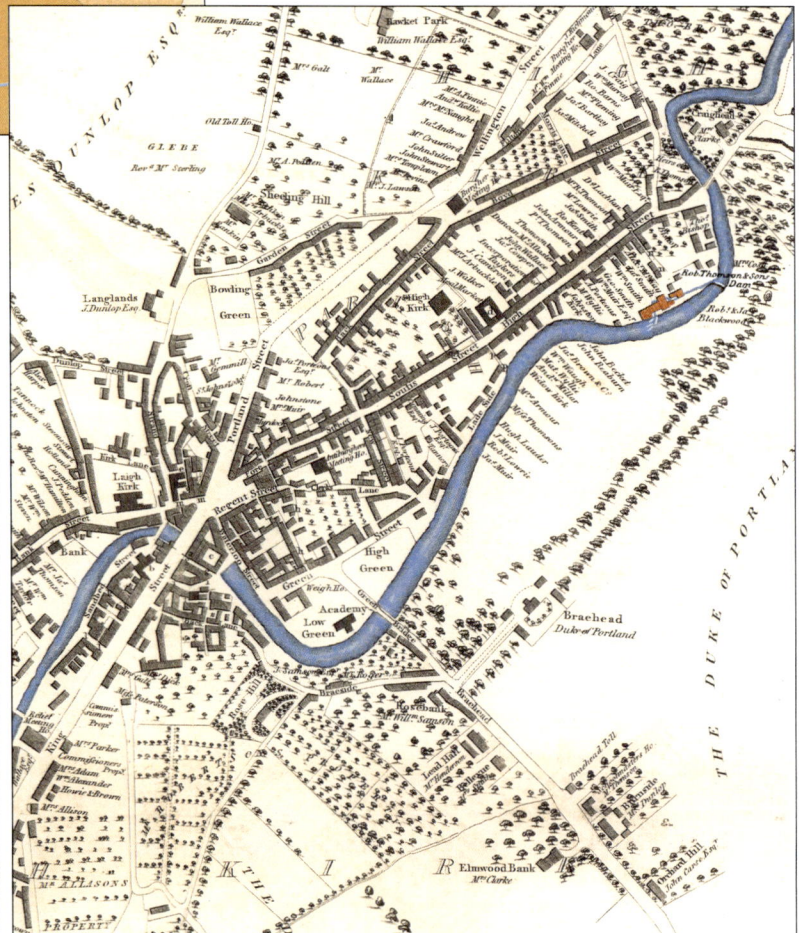

Plan of the Town of Kilmarnock, Surveyed by John Wood, 1819

built near the dam in 1743 called Kilmarnock Woolen Manufactory. In the mid-1700s, William Gregory joined as a partner and it became Wilson, Gregory, and Company. The weaving factory made carpets, blankets, and various types of cloth. Carpets made in Kilmarnock were known for their good quality and intricate designs.

〰

Mr. Gregory had a son, also named William, born in 1742. William Gregory II worked in Glasgow, twenty miles north of Kilmarnock, for a mercantile, or trading company. This company sent him to America in the early 1760s to work at their location in one of Virginia's largest villages, Fredericksburg. The Rappahannock River runs through Fredericksburg, and young George Washington was raised there. William II worked in Fredericksburg for five years as a clerk in the business. He joined the Masonic Lodge there in 1763 and was a member along with George Washington. In September of 1765 William II and his friend William Glen, who was also from Kilmarnock, traveled by horse on a great trip up to Philadelphia, Pennsylvania. The two friends rode on horseback north from Fredericksburg and crossed the Potomac River at today's Route 301 bridge, forty miles south of Alexandria, via Old Hooe's Ferry (pronounced *Hoe*) over to the Piscataway area of Maryland. The ferry was run by Colonel Robert T. Hooe, who owned the land.

In Philadelphia, William II took note in his journal of the market there, prices of goods, and more ships moored than he had ever seen. There was a lot of talk about "stamps" or taxes from Britain. William noticed a large ship from London with armed British Marines. Crazy King George in England had decided to place a hefty tax on his American colonies, which did not go down well, and it was about to lead to the Revolutionary War between Great Britain and America. King George was overweight, as could be seen on British coins which were in wide usage, and not in good health. He went through bouts of rage and hysteria, until he was finally tied down by a forward-thinking physician, which worked very well and even helped him to return to relative sanity for periods of time.

William II and his friend Mr. Glen returned to Fredericksburg a few weeks later in October of 1765. On their return trip, they spent the night in Alexandria, Virginia. Alexandria had only been a town since 1749 or about sixteen years. At the time Alexandria's population was about 1,200 people, including about 260 slaves from Africa. The whole town consisted of only about eight blocks along the river and three blocks inland.

After completing his five years of work, Williams II and his friend William Glen left Fredericksburg and moved to New Haven, Connecticut where they ran a trading company exporting lumber, fish, horses and cattle to the West Indies, and bringing back rum, molasses, and sugar. When the Revolutionary War broke out between America and Great Britain in 1776,

# Gregory Family Tree

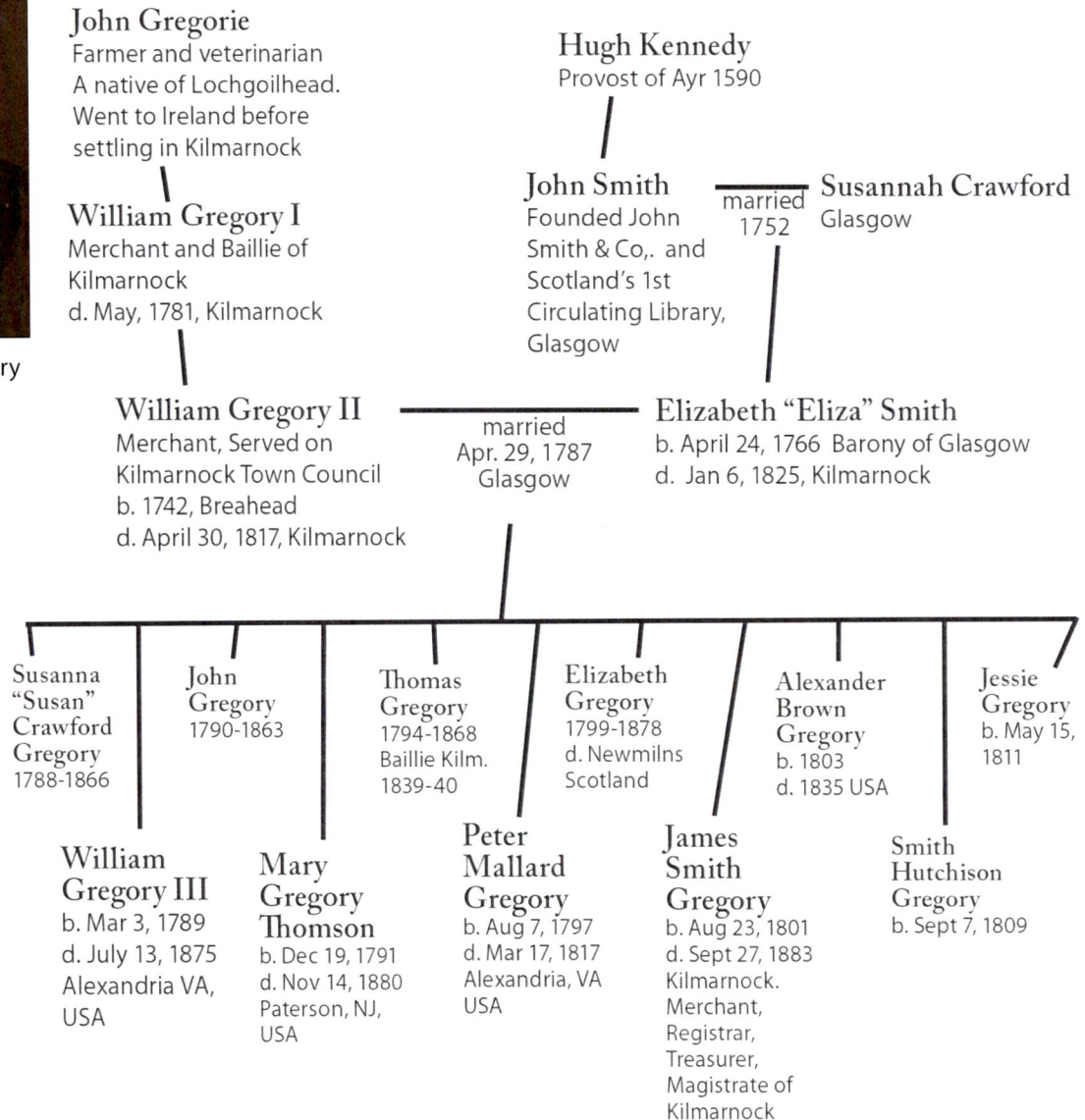

Elizabeth "Eliza" Smith Gregory married William Gregory II in 1787. William III's mother.

**John Gregorie**
Farmer and veterinarian
A native of Lochgoilhead.
Went to Ireland before settling in Kilmarnock

**Hugh Kennedy**
Provost of Ayr 1590

**William Gregory I**
Merchant and Baillie of Kilmarnock
d. May, 1781, Kilmarnock

**John Smith**
Founded John Smith & Co,. and Scotland's 1st Circulating Library, Glasgow

married 1752

**Susannah Crawford**
Glasgow

**William Gregory II**
Merchant, Served on Kilmarnock Town Council
b. 1742, Breahead
d. April 30, 1817, Kilmarnock

married
Apr. 29, 1787
Glasgow

**Elizabeth "Eliza" Smith**
b. April 24, 1766  Barony of Glasgow
d.  Jan 6, 1825, Kilmarnock

**Susanna "Susan" Crawford Gregory**
1788-1866

**John Gregory**
1790-1863

**Thomas Gregory**
1794-1868
Baillie Kilm.
1839-40

**Elizabeth Gregory**
1799-1878
d. Newmilns
Scotland

**Alexander Brown Gregory**
b. 1803
d. 1835 USA

**Jessie Gregory**
b. May 15, 1811

**William Gregory III**
b. Mar 3, 1789
d. July 13, 1875
Alexandria VA, USA

**Mary Gregory Thomson**
b. Dec 19, 1791
d. Nov 14, 1880
Paterson, NJ, USA

**Peter Mallard Gregory**
b. Aug 7, 1797
d. Mar 17, 1817
Alexandria, VA USA

**James Smith Gregory**
b. Aug 23, 1801
d. Sept 27, 1883
Kilmarnock.
Merchant, Registrar, Treasurer, Magistrate of Kilmarnock

**Smith Hutchison Gregory**
b. Sept 7, 1809

A bailie or baillie is a civic officer in the local government of Scotland. The position arose in the burghs, where baillies formerly held a post similar to that of an alderman or magistrate.
— Wikipedia

the two men chose their alliance with their home country and returned home to Kilmarnock, Scotland.

∿

By 1778, William Gregory II was back home in Scotland. The weaving factory owned by his father was located in central Kilmarnock, now the location of the Kilmarnock bus station. A short walk away on Regent Street was an early Gregory family home, which sat on Kilmarnock's central square, on a large intersection of streets. Today this town center is a pedestrian plaza with a statue of poet Rabbie Burns and his publisher John Wilson in the center.

William's father passed away in 1781, and the weaving company continued until 1787 when Mr. Wilson left the business. At that point, the Thomsons came on board, along with William II. The business name was changed to Gregory, Thomson, and Company.

Once established in business, William II married Elizabeth Boyd Smith, called Eliza, in 1787. Eliza's father, John Smith, had a book selling business called John Smith & Company. He founded Scotland's first circulating library in Glasgow. The business became John Smith & Son Ltd., which was located one block from Glasgow's central George Square. The business still operates today as an academic bookseller for Glasgow's universities.

The first child born to William and Eliza was a girl named Susan. The next year, in 1789, their son William Gregory III, our focal point in this book, was born. By the time he was 18 in the year 1807, there were nine children in the family. It was decided that young William would travel to America as his father had done over forty years earlier.

## Union of Great Britain Changes Everything

In the beginning of the 1700s, the most important event in modern Britain's history happened. Scotland and England were combined into one country called Great Britain in 1707. Prior to that, the two countries were mortal enemies and sank each other's ships in naval warfare. That enmity was resolved and it changed the course of human history. Scots were then free to use the waterway without fearing the British Navy, and were able to emigrate to America. Scottish landowners were no longer interested in battling the neighbors. Now the lords wanted nice things and fancy houses.

New ideas for farming came north from England and reached the Lowlands of Scotland first. Better plows were invented and a new method of farming called crop rotation began. Instead of having every family till its soil every year, the idea was to allow fields to lie fallow, which would improve the soil over time. Now landowners needed more crops so they could make more money. Suddenly that scrubby common land between farmtowns became valuable and was needed for

Charles Edward Stuart, "Bonnie Prince Charlie"

The town of Houston in Renfrewshire with houses typically built right up to the sidewalk

larger fields. Big farms were the new thing. People in farmtowns who were barely paying their rent were only in the way. Farmers were sometimes seen as lazy and not caring for their modest dwellings. There was no incentive for the farmers to improve on land they did not own. Now those same people would still be needed seasonally for harvesting the crops for the new larger farms. Workers would be paid a wage for the first time ever, for this seasonal work.

Lairds set about designing and building small towns nearby for their workers. This was the birth of many Lowland Scottish towns of today. In the mid-1700s, landowners in the Lowlands started giving their farmers new twenty-year leases. After twenty years it was understood that families might have to leave their land and move to town. Now roads became a priority so landowners had roads built. Some landowners took great pride in their new towns and roads and felt they were creating a social good. Their town would be attractive. To keep new townspeople from putting the trash heap in front of the house, landowners built the houses right up to the street. All during the 1700s, people were cleared from the land and families moved into towns. This was the beginning of Scotland as we know it.

## The Union Leads to Rebellion

One event caused many people from the northern Highlands of Scotland to leave their family clans and homes and travel south to the Lowlands. But they didn't do it without a fight.

In 1745 many people were still unhappy about the union of English and Scottish parliaments in 1707, making Britain one country. The two countries had been united under one King one hundred years earlier in 1603 under King James VI, but were virtually separate countries until 1707 when Great Britain was formed. Catholic Highland Scots wanted the Catholic James Stuart to depose King George II and become King. James Stuart was called "The Old Pretender" by some. He pretended to be King of Britain while living in exile in Italy. The Latin term for James is Jacob, so followers of James Stuart called themselves "Jacobites" (pronounced *Jack-oh-bites*).

The pretender, James Stuart, was aloof and uninspiring. His son Charles, however, was tall and handsome with red hair and dark eyes. Unlike his father, Charles was energetic and had the ability to inspire. Known as "Bonnie Prince Charlie," Charles plotted to take back the British throne for his father. He marched an army of Scottish peasants south through Scotland into England. Scottish farmers joined the army as it passed by. They were defending the Highland clans' way of life. The Jacobite warriors marched from Catholic-sympathizing northern Scotland, through Presbyterian southern Scotland, and down into England. By the time the men made it halfway into England they were getting homesick. The English people were not inspired to support Charlie's army of Scots, as had been hoped.

The King of Great Britain, George II, sent his son William, Duke of Cumberland, to engage

Prince Charlie's Scottish peasant army marched south into England.

The catholic, James Stuart "The Old Pretender"

Charlie's Scottish forces. Cumberland's soldiers chased Charlie's men back into Scotland, all the way to a place called Culloden (pronounced *Cuh-lawd-en*), near Inverness in the Highlands. Charles had five thousand men who were discouraged, hungry, and tired after an all-night march. Cumberland had nine thousand men. The two armies clashed during a sleet storm. After some Scots were seen fleeing the scene, the remaining Jacobites were pursued and mercilessly slaughtered.

Duane Meyer tells us in his book, *The Highland Scots of North Carolina 1732-1776*, that after the Battle of Culloden, nearly thirty-five hundred Jacobite warriors were taken prisoner. 936 of these men were ordered to leave Scotland. They would escape death and be banished to America. As a result of death, unexpected pardon, or the act of turning King's witness, 142 men escaped their judgment. Records show that 794 Jacobite prisoners were transported to the American colonies. These men were put on ships in shackles and could never return home.

After the Battle of Culloden, everything changed. Wearing a kilt, shoulder belt, or any Highland clothing was banned. Speaking Gaelic (pronounced *gal-ick*) was outlawed. Clan chiefs who had fought at Culloden had their estates confiscated. The family clan way of life was forbidden. Laws were enforced by Sheriff-substitutes who traveled into the Highlands. Many Highland Scots migrated south to the Lowlands of Scotland in search of work.

Meanwhile, dukes, lords, and earls continued to own their castles, palaces, and land. They continued to collect rent. This system continues to this day. The land has been passed down and Scottish landowners still hold these titles, and still collect rent.

A Kilmarnock weaver. From "The Scottish Hand Loom Weavers 1790-1850" by Norman Murray, 1978

Anchor Thread Mill and The Hamills waterfalls, Paisley

## Cotton Revolution Spurs Growth

Scotland was flooded with cheap cotton in the late 1700s. Cotton that was picked by enslaved people was being shipped from America. That cut the price of cotton in half. One might wonder why Americans would sell their cotton so cheaply. If the going rate had been charged, would slavery have even been necessary?

The result of having access to cheap cotton meant that suddenly, money was to be made in Scotland producing cotton fabric! Water wheels on the rivers were converted to powering cotton spinning factories. It was an easy transition to spinning cotton in that part of Scotland because fabric was already being made there. River-powered spinning mills were already making linen from flax plants. Scotland supplied London with its bedsheets or "linens." Water wheels had started out grinding grain for flour. Later, mills might have been used as "waulk" mills for felting wool. Some would be converted for spinning flax, and then to spin cotton.

All over the Lowlands of Scotland, cotton factories were built next to rivers. Over a period of sixteen years, from 1780 to 1796, twenty-seven new factories were built in Renfrewshire in the space of only about one hundred square miles. These were large square-shaped buildings, four to five stories high. They were built of brick or sandstone and had walls three or four feet thick. Visually, they must have dominated the landscape.

Example of a British-made carpet. Photo courtesy of Tetley Workshop, England

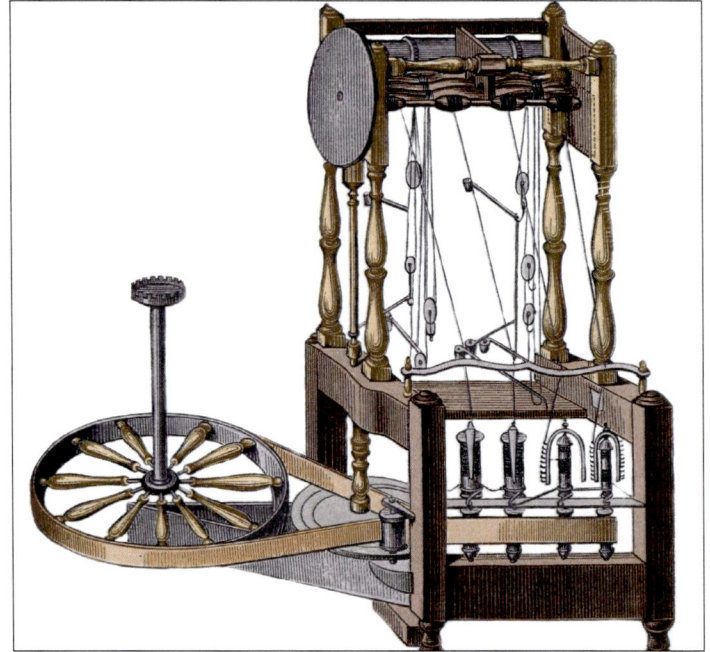

Richard Arkwright's new water-powered cotton spinning frame

Over time, cotton spinning machines were improved. Richard Arkwright invented a new water-powered cotton spinning frame. Weaving looms were gradually improved to weave wider fabric.

With the cotton revolution, workers were now needed in all the new spinning and weaving factories. People flowed into the Lowlands of Scotland for work. The population in some towns doubled every ten years. People moved in from the Highlands, from Ireland, and from England. It was a population explosion! Whole towns were built along the Clyde River. Street grids were laid out and housing was built quickly for the new workers. These buildings housed many people and were called tenements. People worked in thread factories in Paisley. People spun silk in Lochwinnoch. They made cotton in New Lanark. They wove carpets in Kilmarnock. This cotton revolution was as life-changing as today's digital revolution. It changed Scotland forever.

It may be hard to imagine changing from subsistence living to suddenly using money, but from the 1700s on, Scots could not live without money. They could no longer get by with foraging. They lived on their small wage from the factory. People used money for the first time and the free-market economy was born. Trading with England and America was good for Scotland. Some Scots went to university and they had more options. Tobacco coming from America made people in Scotland rich. In 1776, the Revolutionary War broke out between America and Britain. All trading stopped. After the war, Scotland ceased tobacco trading and turned to cotton manufacturing and shipbuilding.

# A Port for Glasgow

The history of Scotland is one of shipbuilding and epic voyages to all parts of the globe. Throughout the ages people traveled to Scotland not by land but by ship. Ships arrived at the town of Greenock (pronounced *Green-ick*), the country's biggest deep port, on the Clyde River. The Clyde was wide and shallow and full of small islands. The city of Glasgow was located twenty-five miles further inland.

Despite being Scotland's second largest city at the time, Glasgow had no access to a deep-water port. It was growing so quickly that it needed lumber, food, tobacco, and sugar for its people. It needed a port on the Clyde deep enough for ships. The problem was resolved in 1668 when landowner Patrick Maxwell, owner of Newark Castle—today one of the best-preserved castles of its time—sold the land around his castle to the city of Glasgow, to become its port and harbor. Thus, the town of Port Glasgow, about twenty-one miles downstream, was born. Goods were taken off the ships at Port Glasgow and moved up-river in smaller boats. A new town grid of streets was laid out, and many people moved to Port Glasgow to work in the shipyards and warehouses.

# Shipbuilding on the Clyde

The Clyde River may be most famous for the many ships built there. Wooden sailing ships were built in Greenock, Port Glasgow, Renfrew, and Paisley. Scott's Family Shipyard opened in

Bleau's Map of 1654. The Clyde River

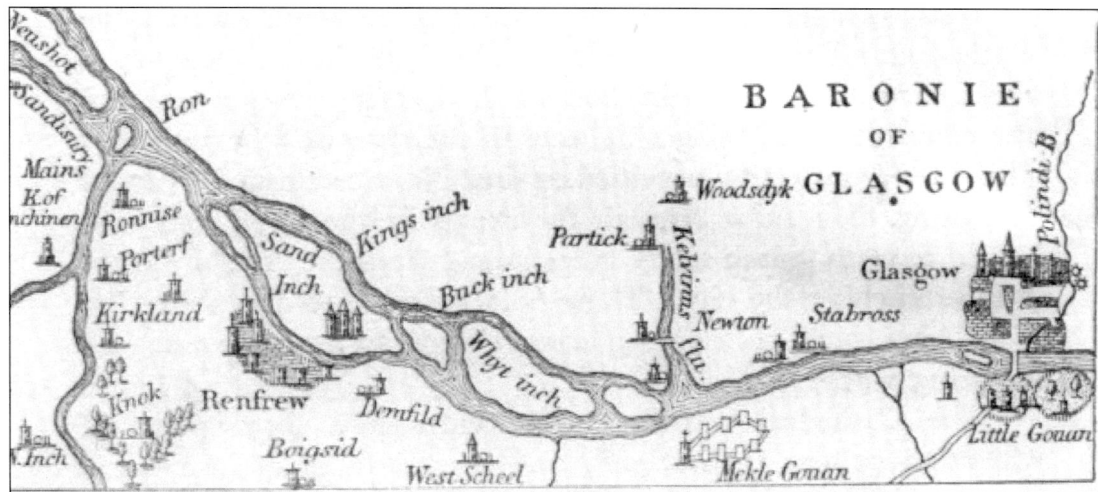

Newark Castle built in 1478 on land that later became Port Glasgow. Behind the castle is a crane from the Clyde region's last shipyard, Ferguson Shipbuilders.

Greenock in 1712. In 1716 the first Clyde-built ship for trade with America was launched from Greenock. Nineteen years later the city of Glasgow owned fifteen ships for trade with Virginia. The first steamship in Scotland, called the *Comet*, was built in 1812 in Port Glasgow. Soon more steamships were being built on the Clyde and used for transport around Britain. A replica of the *Comet* is on display at the Port Glasgow riverfront today.

In the late 1700s, the grand river-dredging project of the Clyde was begun. It was an engineering feat. The Clyde River was so wide and shallow that large ships could travel no further upstream than the town of Port Glasgow. The river dredging dramatically changed the landscape, making the Clyde River much narrower and much deeper. It allowed for large ship construction further upstream, closer to the city of Glasgow. Eventually some of the most famous large ships were built on the river in a growing shipbuilding industry.

From 1707 on, people were able to freely leave Scotland on a ship. This had not been possible before, as England and Scotland had been at maritime war as long as anyone could remember. Scottish ships had not been allowed to enter an English port. When Scotland became part of Great Britain, its ships were protected by the formidable British Royal Navy.

# America Beckons

During the 1700s, families were leaving farmtowns and moving into towns to work as cottage weavers, warehouse workers, or factory workers. Meanwhile, across the Atlantic Ocean, America was being settled. Land was to be had. Letters were coming from relatives about success and opportunity. Articles in the news raved about possibilities in the new land.

To a tenant farmer or a worker in Scotland, this was important news. They could not buy land where they lived. They couldn't own it, so they would never have anything to pass on to their children. However, in America, they could buy land for the same amount of money that they would pay for a year's rent in Scotland. The thought of a better life created a huge incentive to leave and travel to America.

As America beckoned, ships left from every port in Scotland to carry people to the new land. They left from the Firth of Forth and Aberdeen on the east coast. They left from the western islands and from the Clyde River in the west. Where there was a port, ships were carrying people out. By 1776, 150,000 Scots had emigrated to America.

Passengers waiting to board their ship

William Gregory III, 1789-1875

View of the Clyde River from Lyle Hill above Greenock, looking towards the north west

Inventory
  of Wearing Apparel, Books &c March 9th 1807
    Library
Thomson works    4 vol.
Ramsay           2 "
Gay              2 "
Sterne           1 "
Allisons Evidence 1 "
Evergreen        2 "
Poems            2 "
    Music
German Flute & 2 Music Books

2 good new coats
2 "    old "
3 Pairs dark & light pantaloons (Nankin)
2 prs old gray & Blue    ditto do.
1 pr Fine new cloth
5 new vests
3 old do.

    Shirting
12 new day shirts
3 old do.  do.
4 new night do.
2 new neck shirts
10 new neck cloths
2 white pocket handkerchiefs
6 colour'd do.  do.
6 pairs white cotton stockings
3 prs coloured    do.
5 prs woolen    do.

2 prs new shoes
1 pr old shoes
3 prs gaiters
1 cloth brush
1 stuffer
1 pr leather & 1 pr worsted Gloves
2 black neck cloths
1 colour'd do.
2 towels & a pillow-slip
1 twill'd ½ sheet, Mark'd C.L.
2 prs blankets W.G.
A Black & Green Woolen Coverlit
A Mattras & Pillow
        8
An old Fashioned Great Coat

William III's handwritten list of items to take on his journey. Has been cropped to fit.

36

Unfortunately, where there is opportunity, there is the possibility of ne'er-do-wells taking advantage of people. Hucksters made money by selling overpriced tickets for a place on a ship. False promises were made about the length of the journey being shorter than it really was. In the 1700s the journey took up to eleven weeks at sea. Laws had been passed to ensure a minimum of space per person, but laws were hard to enforce. Migrants arrived in America sick, half-starved, and penniless.

If you were one of those immigrants, you could travel in the middle of the ship, called steerage. Steerage was often crowded, damp, and smelly. Illness was common and rats were a problem. You did your own cooking and you might be supplied each week of the voyage with bread, oats, flour, rice, sugar, molasses, tea, pork, and twenty-one quarts of water. Or so it was advertised. More money bought you a cabin above. If you were lucky, you could have one of ten to twenty cabins. You got a bed, linens, a sink, and some drawers for your clothes. Your cabin might open to a communal dining space. Once you had secured your place on board a ship, you had to wait until your ship had enough cargo, people, and the right wind to sail. You might have spent all your money on the fare and now had to survive while waiting. It was a risk—but you were determined to have a better life.

## Leaving Greenock

The port for outgoing ships from the Clyde River was the town of Greenock. Greenock was a growing town, sitting on the southern shore of the Clyde, where the river has always been deep. The northern shore and layered low-lying hills are visible in the distance. Many a painting shows sailing ships moored or sailing out of Greenock. Shortly after leaving Greenock, ships steer southward and into the Firth of Clyde or mouth of the Clyde, and past the Isle of Bute on the right or starboard. The small Cumbrae Island falls away portside to the left. Ships would continue south and past the large Isle of Arran, then past Ireland and out into the Atlantic Ocean.

Greenock's town center is near the waterfront, and the water's edge is bordered by a stone wall where enormous ships can tie up. A customs house was built next to the water for incoming goods. Greenock's waterfront must have been teaming with people and all their luggage, waiting to board their ship. And William was one of them.

## William's Journey Begins

In March of 1807, 18-year-old William Gregory III climbed into a horse-drawn stage coach in Kilmarnock, Scotland. He traveled north and west for thirty-seven miles to Greenock, which took about four hours. His coach rocked and bumped along roads that were newly paved with local whinstone. In Greenock, ships were waiting to sail to America. William had several trunks with him. One trunk held his library. He carried sixteen books, two of them being music books,

William waited in Greenock with a family friend until he could board his ship. By Richard P. Leitch

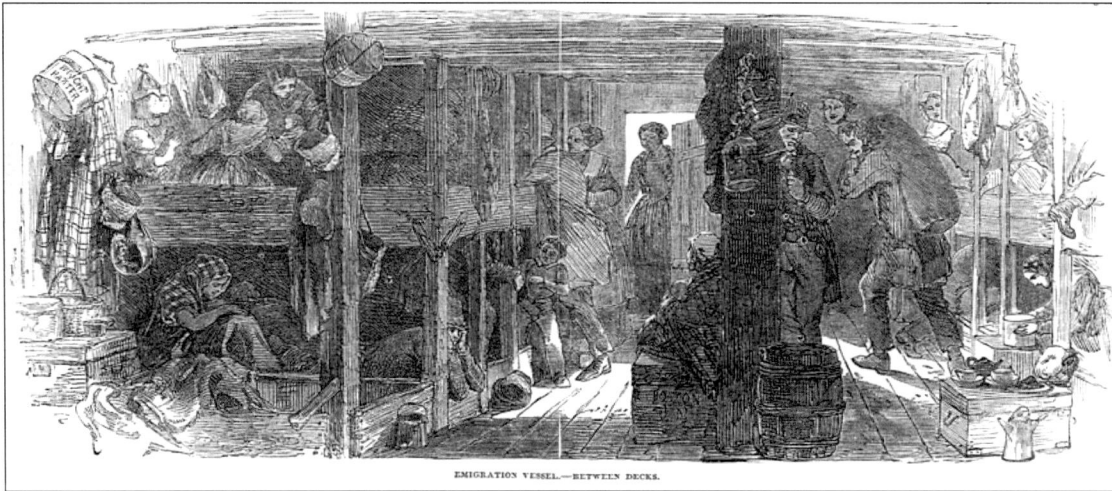

EMIGRATION VESSEL.—BETWEEN DECKS.

Ship passengers in steerage

and a flute. He had a great coat (what we call a trench coat or heavy overcoat), new and old jackets, shirts, cotton stockings, two towels, a pillow, and a mattress.

William stayed in Greenock with a family friend until he could board his ship. He purchased a private cabin aboard a wooden sailing ship called the Ganges. As he entered his small room, William closed his door and fell to his knees at his small bed and prayed for protection on his journey to the new world. On March 21 an easterly wind carried the ship down the Clyde River towards New York City. William wrote a letter that morning to his father:

> To: Mr. Will. Gregory, Merchant, Kilmarnock
> Greenock, March 21st   5 morning   1807
> Dear Father, We are making down the Clyde, and I again embrace this opportunity of writing again. We set sail this morning at 1 o'clock with a fine East wind very unexpectedly & as soon as I arrive I shall write.
> I remain, Dear Father, Your most effectionate son, W. Gregory

It was easy to get into America. Newcomers did not need a passport to enter. People living in America before 1783 were simply American. After 1802, anyone living in the United States for five years was a citizen.

By the time William arrived in America, many years had passed since the end of the American Revolutionary War with Great Britain, and since the term "United States of America" was first used in an American newspaper and became widespread. American coins had the words "United States of America" curled along the coin's edge, and portrayed an image of Lady Liberty with long, flowing hair instead of King George's profile.

William spent the summer in New York City living with Mr. Wilson and looking for work. He wrote to his father on May 22, 1807:

> I have been for this two weeks with a merchant of the name of John Craig… who will need us for about three weeks yet. …He gives me four or five dollars a week which I like better than doing nothing and going about idle. Trade being so dull makes it a great deal worse to get a place… This day I have been assisting Mr. Wilson in his store, he having a great deal to do at this time. The Greenock vessels sailing so near to each other I expect to be able in a day or two to write you of my having got a place. I have nothing further to add only give my best to my mother, brothers and sisters & all Glasgow and Renfrew friends…
> I remain dear Father, Your most obed. Son, Will. Gregory

By "place," he meant a place to work. William didn't get a job right away. He described the summer in New York City and his difficulty finding a job in a letter to his father. He mentioned

Ships landed at Manhattan in
New York City, New York

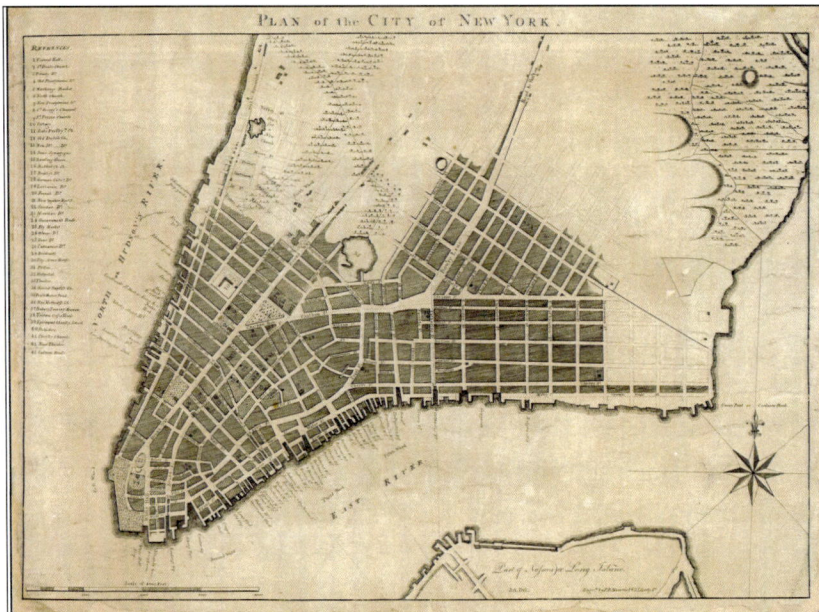

New York in 1796

that his last letter was sent from Liverpool, which was the closest ships port after Greenock, south of Scotland on the English coast, 216 miles from Kilmarnock. Notice that he referred to Scotland as "North Britain":

Mr. William Gregory,
Kilmarnock, N. Britain                                    Alexandria   February 2nd, 1808

Dear Father,
I have now to acknowledge receipt of your two letters the 1st, 2nd Sept. per Mr. Gibson… I wrote you about the last of September via Liverpool informing you of my having got a place in Alexandria. I believe I acted a little imprudently at the first, by going to Craig. I was so keen to get something to do, that I never thought, that by going to him, I had no time left to look out for a more permanent place. When Craig had no more use for me, neither had any other person. Spring trade was over, I saw that I must wait with patience until the Fall. During the Summer I regularly open and shut Mr. Wilson's store, did the most of his writing, went about among every person I knew, told them I had not got a place yet, they all at first promised they would enquire among their friends to do what they could for me.

Fall at last arrives, trade duller than usual & for the affair of the Chesapeake had cast a gloom upon the commercial world. For one half of the Fall orders were not executed. I then thought it was high time to bestir myself, depend no more on the promises of friends. I went and began at one end of a street and continued to the other, going into and enquiring at almost every store - still that was unavailing, for they all sung the same tune.

I got word at last from a real friend of a merchant that wanted a young man, that he would prefer me, being a countryman of his; I went to him and was with him about 2 weeks when I engaged with Mr. McCrea. I left New York about the first October. Was in Philadelphia 3 days, was in Baltimore, and passed through Washington, at which place I have been often since, it being about 6 miles above Alexandria. Every time I am up, I always spend an hour or two in Congress to hear the debates.

## Heading South to Alexandria

In 1807, when William found his way from New York City to Alexandria, he was 18, looking for work in a strange country, and on his own. People at that time traveled from city to city by horse-drawn stagecoach. It would take a whole day to get from one city to another. So people would stop and stay in one city for a few days and visit friends. You might spend about a week to get from New York City to Alexandria. You would stop off in Philadelphia, Baltimore, and

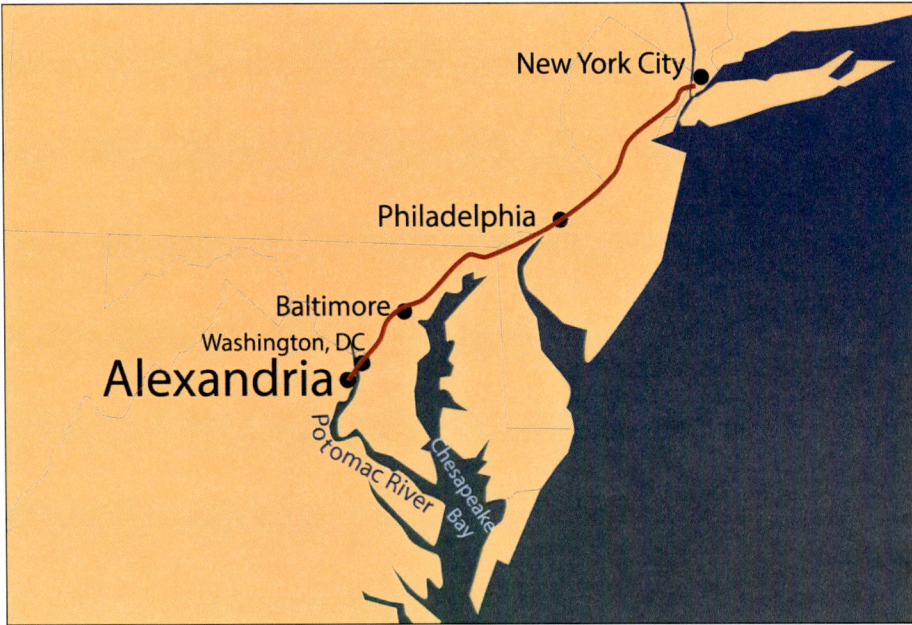

William's journey from New York City to Alexandria took almost a week.

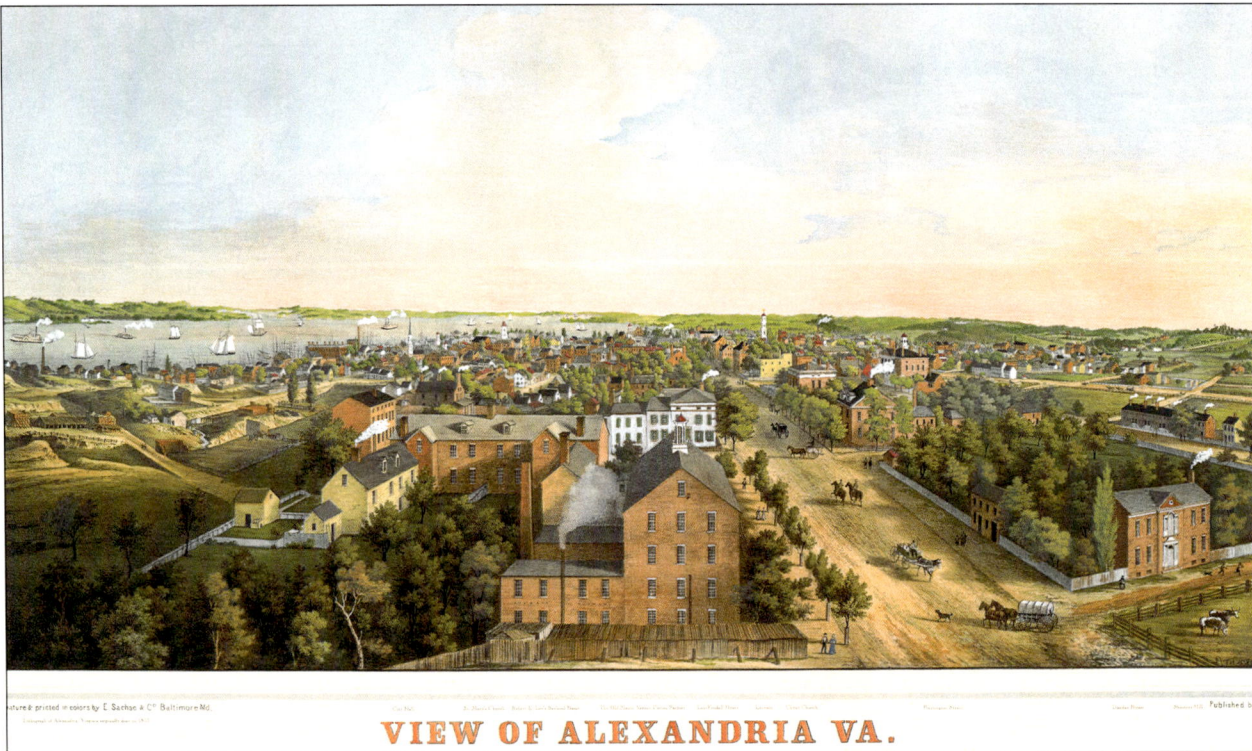

VIEW OF ALEXANDRIA VA.

View of Alexandria from the north, looking down Washington St. The cotton factory is center front. William's house is beyond that, the small brick one behind the white Lee home. Hand-colored print, courtesy of Todd Healy.

Washington, D.C. Today's twenty-minute drive from Washington, D.C. to Alexandria took two hours by water. Your entire stagecoach, horse, and travelers would cross the Potomac River on a ferry boat.

The city of Alexandria is on the west side of the Potomac. In 1807 it was part of Washington, D.C. and was called Alexandria, D.C. Going inland from the Chesapeake Bay, about ninety miles up the Potomac River, Alexandria is the last deep port. People arriving in Alexandria soon found out that life was hard. Illness arrived with people coming in on ships. There were bouts of terrible sickness that would run through Alexandria. The waterfront south of the city had to be set up as a quarantine and many people died.

Although Alexandria was part of Washington, D.C, it was separated by the wide and deep Potomac River. That meant there was not much rule of law and citizens took matters into their own hands. Houses were mostly made of wood so if your house caught on fire, you called on one of the citizen-run fire companies. You were lucky if anyone arrived to put your fire out! Some buildings were made of local brick. A few of the streets were paved with cobblestones but most were choppy gravel and mud.

William and all his cases arrived in Alexandria in October of 1807. His new position was at the dry goods business called Robert McCrea & Company. The store was at the corner of South Fairfax Street and Prince Street. Robert McCrea probably walked the half mile to welcome William at the ferry terminal at the foot of Oronoco Street. Later William proudly told his brother how he had carried all his own luggage to his new home.

Robert McCrea's store in Alexandria sold fabrics, bedding, carpet, linens, flannel, hats, silk, cording, and sheets brought by ship to New York City from London, Italy, Germany, and Ireland. These goods did not arrive at Alexandria's port on the Potomac River. There was more to it than that. Goods from other countries arrived in New York City. Someone had to be there to see the goods arriving, buy them, and transport them back to Alexandria over a period of several days in a horse-drawn carriage. Mr. McCrea needed someone he could trust to manage his shop while he was off buying products. A young man from his home country of Scotland could suit that need, so William was a perfect fit.

When new products arrived at the store, Mr. McCrea would place an advertisement in the local newspaper, the *Alexandria Gazette*. His ad would be printed on a letterpress printing machine, using metal type and ink on paper. Pages from the *Alexandria Gazette* going all the way back to William's time are available at the Kate Waller Barrett Branch Library in Alexandria. We can read Robert's ads and see the news that William was reading.

William had his first look at his new home—Alexandria—in October of 1807. In a letter

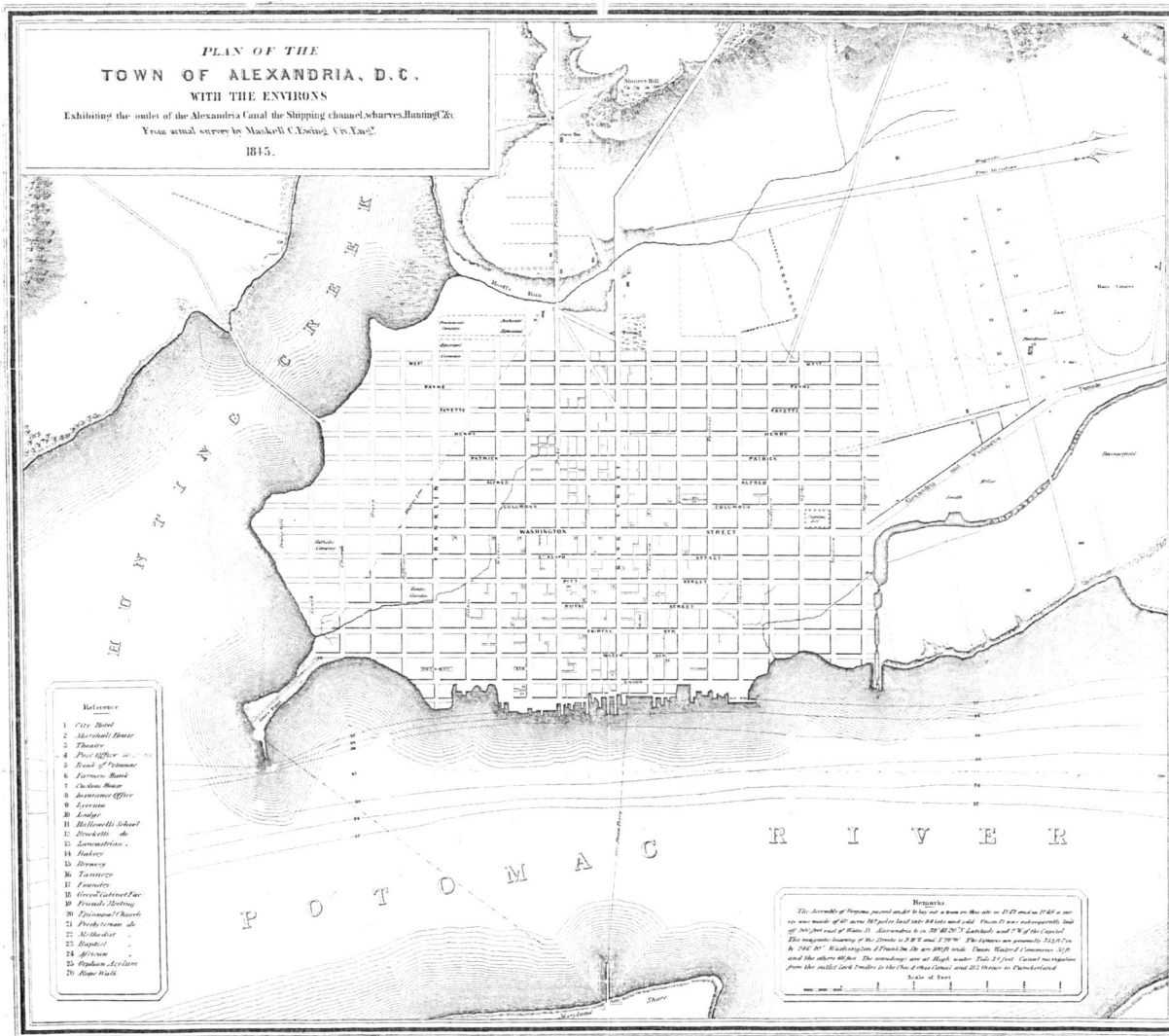

Map of Alexandria, D.C., 1845. From Alexandria Library, Barrett Branch, Local History Special Collections

to his father on February 2, 1808, William wrote about his first impressions of this American town. It may not be clear to today's reader, but the number "3" here is meant to be read as *three thousand*:

> Alexandria is a pretty large town, very regular laid out. It contains about 8 thousand inhabitants, 3 of them negros. The river Potomac is navigable for a 50 gun ship to Washington, or small craft a good way further. I have got into a very good situation, I believe among well doing people.

Other sources say that Alexandria's population was over six thousand in the year 1800. The

U.S. Census, which counts all people, reported that Alexandria's population was 7,227 in 1810, with 68 percent being white, 12 percent free blacks, and 20 percent enslaved black people. This place was clearly growing. Across the Potomac River, Washington, D.C. had only about one thousand more people at 8,200, and Georgetown, which is part of Washington today, had just under 5,000 people.

Another person who had also visited Alexandria around that same time had written: "Alexandria is one of the most wicked places I ever beheld in my life. Cock fighting, horse racing, with every species of gambling, cheating being apparent…"

William had a similar impression about the city. Notice that he used the word *Fredericksborough* for Fredericksburg, which shows that he pronounced it the same way as the word *Edinburgh* is pronounced in Scotland:

> The natives of this country are for the most part very irreligious. They sing, dance, play at cards and all other games on Sunday. It is the only day they set aside to decide their bets. There were no less than about 30 profest gamblers here during the Races. Fredericksborough was mostly burnt at its last races. Some people compare it to ancient Sodom that was burnt for its wickedness.

## The Birth of Alexandria

The town of Alexandria was created nearly sixty years before young William arrived. Here's a bit of the backstory. Scottish-born John Alexander purchased land by the Potomac River and Hunting Creek from prominent feminist and landowner Margaret Brent, an English immigrant, in 1669. Alexander was a tobacco farmer like most European settlers in the area, so he paid for the land with tobacco. After John Alexander's death, part of his land along the river and next to a wide bay passed to a man named Hugh West.

The shores of the Potomac River were shallow so a sturdy structure was needed, bigger than a pier, to reach into the deep part of the river so ships could tie up and receive *hogs heads*—large barrels of tobacco—from surrounding farms. Hugh West built such a structure called a wharf near a high bluff by the bay in 1732. Near his wharf he built a warehouse to serve as a tobacco inspection point for the area. Hugh West also ran a ferry and a tavern there. Shipping was so important to the local economy that local merchants asked the government of Virginia to establish a town at West's warehouse.

So in 1749 the town of Alexandria, Virginia was born. George Washington was 17 years old at the time. He helped lay out the town's street grid with Hugh's son, John West, the deputy surveyor of the new Fairfax County. The wharf and its buildings were called West's Point, and

Alexandria's waterfront in the 1800s. From Alexandria Library, Local History Special Collections.

are now the southern end of Oronoco Bay Park. *Oronoco* was the name of the tobacco that was stored at West's warehouse for inspection. The tobacco was loaded onto ships to be taken to Scotland.

When William arrived in 1807, Alexandria's early generation of Scottish settlers were either aged, or had passed on, like William Ramsay and John Carlyle—both founding trustees of the town. Alexandria's first mayor, from 1780 to 1781, Robert T. Hooe (pronounced *Hoe*) was about 63 years old and would die two years later. It was Hooe's family who had owned the ferry forty miles south on the Potomac River where William's father and William Glen had crossed on their trip to Philadelphia in 1763. Scottish-born James Muir was minister at the church William attended, the Presbyterian Meeting House on South Fairfax Street. James Muir, age 51 at the time, was born in the southern Scottish county of Ayrshire, the same county where Kilmarnock lies.

Alexandria's City Hall was, and still is, a large red brick building. It faced Cameron Street, which was the city's main street, running east–west from the river. City Hall was then also the Alexandria Market House. Behind City Hall in what is now Market Square, the block was filled with one- and two-story buildings with alleyways running between them where the Farmer's Market took place. A visitor in 1808 described Alexandria's market: "There is here open every morning, an abundantly supplied market with all kinds of meat and every species of vegetables."

That Farmer's Market remains a popular weekly event today. Along the south side of Market Square runs King Street, which is now Alexandria's main commercial street. From Market Square and the corner of Fairfax Street, King Street takes a dive down a gentle slope, three blocks to the edge of the river. At one point, Native Americans stood on a path at the top of that slope, which was much steeper then, and looked out at swamp and a wide river beyond. In the 1700s much effort was taken to fill in the swamp and extend King Street to the point where more wharves could be built to accommodate ships. Alexandria was a hard-scrabble working town. The shoreline was lined with warehouses and wharves where commodities were loaded onto ships like tobacco and later wheat, and human slaves.

## Waiting for Letters

Keeping in touch with family in Europe was very difficult for new Americans. Letters took two months to arrive, over sea and land. William waited impatiently for letters from home. He wrote a letter to his father on April 4, 1808, which didn't arrive until June 2. It was sent via Lord Kobbart, who operated the Atlantic route between 1805 and 1820. In the letter, he mentioned his brother John, his employer Mr. McCrea (who was preparing to make purchases from ships arriving from Europe), and the high cost of goods:

pr. British packet
Lord Kobbart.
Mr. William Gregory
Merchant
Kilmarnock, Scotland                                    Alexandria 4th April, 1808

I have to acknowledge receipt of your letter incl. one from John. Also one from Mr. W. Smith, so far back as October last. I understand by your letter, he has since sailed for Granada, as Mr. McCrea sets out for New York today. And the British Packet sails in the course of a fortnight, I am not willing to lose the opportunity, as it will be the only one for some length of time.

I was very happy to hear by your letter that you were all well, as I had not heard from you for some time before. Business is now very dull and all sorts of dry good dear, those included in the Non-Importation Act are a great deal higher. Thread are up to nearly double their former value. Linens and Fine Cloth are also much… I am sorry to hear of business being so dull for you but Kilmarnock is not the only place that will suffer. The Irish will feel it as much as any, for they export a great deal of linens to this country and the regular supply of flax seed that they had from this country was stopt.

Wishing you better times, I am your affectionate son, William Gregory
Came to hand June 2, 1808. [This notation shows the date the letter was received.]

During William's first year in Alexandria, William's father wrote and asked if he could ship carpets to Alexandria. Unfortunately, the 1807 embargo kept goods from coming in from Britain until the summer of 1810. This trade embargo was imposed by President Thomas Jefferson in December, 1807, shortly after William arrived in Alexandria. The embargo was in response to troubles at sea over the war between Britain and France in the Napoleonic Wars.

William was used to the weather in Scotland being moderate year-round, never very hot, and cold and dark in winter but not much snow. So during his first summer in Alexandria, William wrote on July 16, 1808: "We have now very warm weather, the thermostat has been from 86 to 96 for these three weeks by past."

William witnessed an important event for Alexandria—the building of the "Long Bridge" over the Potomac River, from just north of Alexandria to Washington, D.C. This bridge was built of wood for pedestrians and horse-drawn stage coaches. It took about one year to build and opened in May of 1809. Its original purpose was to speed mail delivery between the two cities. At that time there was no door-to-door mail delivery, and the post office was wherever the postmaster lived. William picked up his mail at the home of Post Master George Gilpin, whose house and post office was at 208 King Street. Years earlier, a Robert McCrea had been postmaster from 1776 to 1791. This may have been Mr. McCrea or his father.

## New Partnerships

McCrea & Company did not have to rely only on Europe for their fabrics. In the spring of 1809, McCrea entered into a partnership with Mr. McMaster of Wilmington, North Carolina, for receiving fabrics made in that state. Like Alexandria, Wilmington was a major eastern seaport. McCrea traveled to Wilmington, located on the Cape Fear River, and brought back cotton fabric made in North Carolina. It sold well in Alexandria. William wrote:

Mr. McCrea is at present in North Carolina. He exchanges goods for cloth manufactured there, which sells very quick here, as the people are becoming so patriotic that they will wear nothing but that which is manufactured of the US.

Mr. McCrea gave William a pay raise to $250 per year, in addition to "bed, board and washing."

President Jefferson's trade embargo against British goods lasted until the summer of 1810. However, business had started to pick up by the spring for McCrea's dry goods store. In March of 1810 William wrote home about the status of the business. His disappointment about the continued lack of communication with his family is clear:

Dear Father,

The last letter I have from you is dated 11th September - that I should be so long without any intelligence from your quarter is a matter of some surprise to me who have always been punctually dealt with that way… I continue in very good health at present. Business at present is tolerably brisk and as the spring advances will get brisker. All sorts of linen goods are amazing high & cotton goods as low as ever. Has the factory company as many American orders as they used to have? Do they still keep as many looms going as formerly? The improvements of your town must be greatly advanced by this time and I can almost fancy myself a stranger in it.

A new partner named Mr. McGill was brought into McCrea & Company. Unfortunately McGill turned out to be a gambler who brought nothing to the business but debt. One day in January of 1812, Mr. McCrea left the shop in William's hands, and went to New York City with McGill to dissolve the partnership. William wrote about his hope to maintain his working relationship with Mr. McCrea:

Mr. William Gregory, Merchant, Kilmarnock, N. Britain

Alexandria,  10 January, 1812

Dear Father,

I wrote you about the 1st December last acknowledging receipt of your letter of 17 Sept. enclosing one from Peter. I have not wrote to Susan, Mary and Eliza and shall write Peter in a little time. Robert McCrea and J. McGill are on their way to New York, where it is the intention of R. McCrea immediately to demand a settlement and close the business. I am left here to sell off what few goods are remaining on hand and collect outstanding debts.

My chief motive for writing to you at present is knowing that if trade is again renewed with Britain it is McCrea's intention to begin business again and probably in this place. I would beg the favour of you immediately to write to him on my behalf, as offered to do above one year ago. If he does open here I conceive that I have a better chance than any other person, especially as I am well acquainted with the town, with their customers, with their books which I for some years past have kept, and he nor no one else can reproach me with gambling, keeping bad company, drunkeness or of keeping untimeous hours. I profess to be as competent to do business and as well acquainted with goods etc as others who have had the like experience - I settled with the concern up to the New Year and had a balance in my favour of $522.

I wrote Thomas about 3 weeks, I am really surprised at his silence, never having had but one letter from him, and that came about ten days after I wrote him my first.

McCrea's ostensible motive in taking McGill to New York, is to sail for Britain immediately for the purpose of purchasing goods to be in time for the opening of trade; his real intention is to bring about a Settlement with him, having given me possession of the Books, notes, etc here and having the Bills of Exchange redrawn in favour of himself, he will be enabled to bring things to a hearing and right himself for the sums of money that McGill lost by gambling, keeping much company etc. and probable loss by his non-attendance to his business - if he [McGill] goes across the water (which is a question with me whether he will, or not, when he knows his fate) he will likely call upon you and I beg you will shew him that attention which you would to any one who had befriended me. He will likely want some carpeting, but I should not wish that anything I have wrote, operate as a recommendation. Expecting to hear from you as soon as convenient.
I remain Dear Father, Your most affectionate Son, Wm. Gregory
P.S. I have wrote the foregoing very hastily having several others to write before the Closing of the Mail. WG
P.S. McCrea is not such a man as the other, but is a steady, sober, active man and is in as good credit as any person can be, buys most of his goods for Cash at Vendue and has a super eminent advantage over any other Merchant in the same time in this place.

As it turned out, William had nothing to worry about, as Robert McCrea had every intention of keeping him on. When Mr. McCrea returned to Alexandria, he reopened the dry goods store in a new partnership with William. William was 23 years old and had been supporting himself for about five years. He immediately wrote home to his father to order carpets from the factory in Kilmarnock:

Mr. McCrea offered me one third of the profits of the Store henceforth if I choose to remain. I have of course agreed and at his request have wrote for some Carpeting from Gregory, Thomson & Co.

Along with all the changes in the business, William was also affected by an event of nature. A series of earthquakes occurred in New Madrid, Missouri, in late 1811 and up until February of 1812. The earthquakes rattled Alexandria and caused William to write to his parents:

> We have extremely cold weather. The ink is freezing in the pen. We have had frequent shocks of earthquakes lately. This morning one was very sensibly felt. It stopped clocks and set things that were suspended from the ceiling knocking one against the other.

Within a short time, he would experience the effects of war.

# Defending Alexandria in the War of 1812

In Alexandria, all men between ages 18 and 45 were required to join the militia. They provided their own blue uniforms and were assigned to a company of one hundred men. They would drill with their unit once a month. Alexandria had an empty field where the men would drill on the west side of North Washington Street, which was called "the catalpa lot" because of the surrounding catalpa trees there.

British ships in the Atlantic Ocean continued to board American ships with impunity and *impress* or simply take American sailors and force them to serve in the British war against the French. Over six thousand seamen were impressed into British service. This enraged the American public. James Madison was now president. Congress declared war against Great Britain in June of 1812 even though the American Navy was fledgling and unprepared for battle.

Alexandria's part and William's participation in the War of 1812 actually took place in the summer of 1814. William and his militia were sent to positions south of Alexandria on the Potomac River at a place called White House Landing, known today as Fort Belvoir. That position was chosen because it was on a forty-foot high bluff overlooking the river. Ships arriving from the south could be easily spotted.

A sea of billowing sails made their way toward Alexandria in late August, 1814. The fleet of British ships from the world's largest navy sailing up the expansive Potomac River must have been an awesome and shocking sight. Five canons that had been placed along Alexandria's riverbank and most of the artillery had been removed to the Maryland side of the river, leaving Alexandria defenseless. City leaders knew the town was doomed, so a delegation of three men rowed south to meet the British Commander and negotiate terms of surrender. These terms were refused, and that evening the British ships arrived at Alexandria. Overnight they pointed one hundred thirty-eight guns towards the small wood and brick town.

Alexandrians had known the British were coming, so a great effort had been made to move

Troops at White House Landing on the Potomac River at today's Fort Belvoir. Above the White House Battery flew a flag emblazoned with "FREE TRADE & SAILOR'S RIGHTS." Sketch by William Bainbridge Hoff, Naval Historical Center

goods out to the countryside. The British, who were severely low on provisions, demanded Alexandria's ships and any food, tobacco, and supplies. Alexandria's town council complied and over five days British sailors came into Alexandria and went door-to-door to retrieve their loot. They were described as being courteous, but they made off with twenty-one of Alexandria's ships loaded with the city's flour, tobacco, and raw cotton. Goods were taken from warehouses, and Alexandria's docks were burned.

As the fleet of ships and boats left Alexandria and retreated south down the Potomac River, William and the other soldiers up on the hill could see them coming. As the convoy approached the bluff, the wind changed direction and slowed the ships. This left the battleships vulnerable, allowing the Americans to fire at the convoy. Three days of vicious bombing ensued and William's battery was shelled by the ships. Their heavy iron guns extended out the side of the ships, so all the weight had to be moved to one side, allowing the guns to point upward toward the high cliff. The Americans returned fire and held off British attempts to land ground forces for several days. On September 5, the wind changed course and the convoy retreated down the Potomac River.

# Help from a Brother

Even before Alexandria's conflict with British ships of war, William's employer Robert McCrea was in need of additional help in his store. He wrote a letter to William's father in Kilmarnock asking if another of his sons could travel to America to help out. However, travel from Kilmarnock was put on hold due to the War of 1812. On December 22, 1813, William wrote to his father about Peter joining him in Alexandria:

> In your last letter you mention that as soon as an adjustment takes place between our two Countrys, you intend to send out Peter to me, if it is quite agreeable to him, it will be no less so to me. He will I have no doubt suit us extremely well. In case of his coming he shall experience every encouragement that a brother is entitled to look for. If you have not spoke to him on the subject, you may, the better to know his mind respecting it. …

> I am sorry that the present situation of our Countries prevents a correspondence between us, at a future day we may be of mutual service to each other, as Alexandria exports vast quantities of produce to the West Indies Islands.

When William left Kilmarnock in 1807, there were nine children in the Gregory household: Susan, William, John, Mary, Thomas, Peter, Elizabeth, James, and Alexander. By 1815 their mother Eliza Gregory had had two more children, Smith and Jessie. Their sixth child, Peter, was 17 years old. He would cross the Atlantic Ocean and join his older brother in Alexandria.

In April of 1815, Peter Gregory traveled to Greenock, as William had eight years earlier. Continuing the family interest in music he carried a violin with him, and he was given many letters to take across. In those days you didn't book your ship and show up with your ticket. It was up to Peter to secure a space on a ship. It took several tries for Peter to find a ship that would take him.

Peter wrote his father two letters while he stayed in Greenock, primarily commenting on ship accommodations and cost, and sending best wishes to the family and his siblings:

> Mr. William Gregory, Merchant, Kilmarnock
>
> Greenock  7th April, 1815
>
> Dear Father,
> I would have wrote you sooner had I had my passage agreed for - Mr. McLellan and I went to the agents of the *Mary Ann*, but they would not take me, either in steerage or cabin - because there were no passengers going by her and they would not take a single one. I was therefore obliged to go by the *Independence*. The *Mary Ann* had very bad accommodation in the cabin at any rate - I could not stand upright, the roof was

so low - she likewise is a very old vessel.

The *Independence* is a beautiful ship and has capitol accommodation in the cabin which I was obliged to take, for they would take no steerage passengers. But I believe Mr. McLellan will get a considerable deduction made in the passage money - I do not know as yet what my passage will be, but before I close this perhaps I will know. I have staid in Mr. McLellan's since I had came here. He has been very kind and has paid a great deal of attention to me. I have been several times also at Mr. Wilson's who is likewise very kind.

The *Independence* has cleared out and will sail this day. I have been with the Captain [W. Brown] several times - and I think as yet he is not a Devil. To all appearances he is a very discreet man. There were 7 West India ships arrived here yesterday and we are looking for Americans [American ships] daily.

April 8th, 1815
Owing to something which I cannot explain, the *Independence* ran aground yesterday in the harbour, but I see this morning that she has got out into the stream and as soon as it is full tide, she'll go down - the wind is very calm, but it is fair - I expect to be out the river before dinner.

Mr. McLellan has told me that he spoke to the Glasgow agents about my passage but that they would not say positively whether they would make it less than 40 Guineas - but Mr. McLellan thinks that they will get some deduction. My share of stores is five guineas less than any of the rest of the passengers on account of my not drinking much spirits - which will help a little, I think. The worst of it will be 57.15 pounds - but Mr's W. and Mc. will give you the account. I was so much disappointed in my passage in the *Mary Ann*, that I was determined to go by the *Independence* if they would take me although I should have paid the passage myself.

After I have got settled in America & find it convenient I will remit as much as pay my passage I think. Surely William will not hesitate to advance as much - if he does not I will remit pr. the first opportunity (it will only be keeping my nose to the grindstone for a year or so).

I do not expect that this letter will lye upon the brace for everybody's inspection. You can read it to Mother. Farewell, wishing you health & happiness till I come back - mind me to all the weans [wee ones].

I am dear Father, Your afft. Son, Peter M. Gregory
P.S. I received your letter & Factory's, P.M.G.

Just going to sail. Before you get this I will be passing [the Isle of] Arran.

Finally Peter began his journey to America, writing his father again as he passed by Cumbrae, the first island leaving the Clyde River estuary:

April 8th, 1815
Saturday night, 6 O'Clock off Cumbray.
Dear Father,

I cannot let this opportunity slip without recking my conscience. We sailed from Greenock about 11 o'clock and the wind has been fair ever since, which will enable us to be a good way on by tomorrow - if the wind keeps fair till then. There are 6 passengers besides me - and one of them is particularly acquainted with Mr. McCrea. He says, I saw William Brown - [of the Scottish farm] Busbie in Greenock this day, he has given me some letters to his friends. He goes up to Glasgow this evening but I had nothing to send with him, only to mention to Mary that it was quite out of my power to call upon her - at any rate I expected to have been up at Glasgow and I was not so anxious at that time.

Mr. Smith my Uncle would have made me a present of a pair of bibles had I not had a pair before. John gave me a very neat edition of Burns Poems, which I was much obliged to him for.

You may tell everybody that I got letters from, when you see them, that it was with great difficulty I could get them saved, for they are so strict. Everybody that had letters had to pay 10d for each at the post office before you could take them aboard. But I got my trunk aboard without being inspected - and that saved all the letters.

I have not time to say more, the pilot is just going, and the gentleman by which this goes to Greenock with him.
Give my compliments to all enquiring friends and farewell again,
I remain your Afft. Son, P.M. Gregory

Peter Gregory arrived in Alexandria on June 1, 1815 after almost two months of travel. His ocean passage cost thirty-five guineas. A guinea was a gold coin with an image of King George III in profile. At the time, King George in Britain was going mad. He had lost the colonies in America because of his unreasonable taxations.

Peter worked in the dry goods store. William was happy with Peter's work, writing home to his father in July of 1815, one month after Peter's arrival:

Peter is in good health and spirits and seems so far to be very well pleased with his situation. He is already quite active in the Store - we give him a very good salary. Indeed much beyond what he expected - so that he will not only have it in his power to keep himself in genteel apparel but to lay past a little if so disposed.

Peter was paid $200 per year, plus bed, board, and laundry. Peter had been helping in the store for over a year when in early 1817 William began planning his first trip home to Scotland in ten years. Peter wrote home to his sister Susan about William's upcoming trip, as well as their lack of prospects for marriage:

> Feb 1st, 1817
> Dear Susan,
> Although I wrote a few lines to you 15th last November and that was the last opportunity I had till this and the last letter I wrote home, I could not think of writing all the family without sending you a few lines also.
>
> You will now have a glance of William who leaves this on Monday on his way to Kilmarnock he intents to be back in Alexandria about the 1st July, therefore as I said before you will only get a glance of him. However I hope you may all have a happy meeting with him, when he does arrive. …
>
> William is a complete old bachelor. It is likely he will remain so unless there be some girl (alias old maid) in Kilmarnock that he will fancy. I see no prospect of his being married soon. I would not wish for a better joke than to hear of his bringing over a Scotch wife. As for myself I don't think ever I'll be married, for there are none hereabouts would have me, and as my mother us'd to tell me I would never get one in Kilmarnock. I suppose I'll have to want. I'll leave off with my compliments to all my old friends … my female acquaintances not excepted.
> Believe me I Remain, Your affectionate Brother, Peter M. Gregory

This would be Peter's last letter home.

# William's Visit Home

In late February of 1817, William began his first trip home to Scotland. He traveled first to New York City, and on March 2, he boarded a ship called *Aeolus*, which was headed to Londonderry, Ireland. From there he planned to take the first ship to be found, for Scotland.

The joy of being home and seeing his parents, new and old siblings, and the many changes in Kilmarnock and at the factory must have been intense. During that time however, joy was tempered by grief. Peter had become ill with pneumonia while William was on his way to New York City.

Information was passed along from one person to another, to get word to the family. A man named William Wallace was in New York, looking after Mr. McCrea's business dealings there. Mr. Wallace wrote to the Gregorys in Kilmarnock that William was traveling on the *Aeolus*, and that he, Wallace, had received a letter from John Ramsey in Alexandria saying that Peter had "taken ill with a bilious complaint."

William's friend Andrew Jamieson in Alexandria informed William in a letter written in March:

Alexa Saturday 22nd March 1817

Mr. Wilm. Gregory,
My Dear Young Friend,

I regret being the messenger of heavy tidings but may the god of all grace, mercy and peace give you and your parents strength to bear your affliction & to say in submission to the divine will the Lord gave and the Lord hath taken away Blessed be his name.

I have seen Mr. Auld's letter to you on this heart-rending subject vis the death of the amiable youth your Brother on Monday Morning last and feel for you and your parents although they be strangers to me. Oh that this gloomy and alarming dispensation may be a warning to you and all your young friends (of whom you have many in this place) that you all may be led to consider the uncertainty of life and all its enjoyments God has in his wisdom written vanity and change on us all…

It must be some consolation to your Parents that their Son left no Enemies behind him & none can say that he was a Son that caused shame but his sudden call awakened the feelings of all his neighbors & friends & they seemed to vie with one another who should show most attention & kindness. On this occasion the Revd Dr. Muir of his own accord has offered to Preach a Funereal sermon as an admonition to the Young.

My Wife and Son join Me in Sincere Wishes for your welfare and safe return.
I am dear Sir, your affectionate friend, Andw Jamieson

Pneumonia had taken Peter's life quickly. He died on March 17, 1817. Peter Mallard Gregory is buried in the Presbyterian Cemetery in Alexandria. He was 19 years old.

## Two Brothers Arrive

With Peter's unexpected death, William knew that more help would be needed at the store in Alexandria. So when William returned to Alexandria in the summer of 1817, he had his

16-year-old brother James with him. One source says that James traveled in steerage and paid 12 pounds, 12 shillings for his fare, so it is possible both men rode in steerage on this trip.

After living in Alexandria for a time, James moved across the Potomac River to Washington, D.C. to open his own dry goods store. The move was made easy by the new regular steam ferry service across the Potomac River. The ferry boats when William arrived in 1807 were horse-powered paddle boats. 1n 1815 steam paddle boats were introduced. By 1819 three steamboats serviced the journey from Alexandria to Washington, D.C. or Georgetown, then a neighborhood of Washington.

In 1822, with James in Washington, William's brother Alexander, two years younger than James, traveled to Alexandria to work in the store with William. Writing home from Washington, James noted that he would travel by steamship to Alexandria on Sundays to visit his brothers. The steamship took one hour for the journey. James commented on how Americans were out and about on Sundays, which was unusual in Scotland where rigorous church attendance was required.

The Bartleman home at 207 King St.

It was a busy year. Not only did Alexander arrive from Scotland, but also there was a wedding! At the age of 33, William finally found a wife. Margaret Bartleman, daughter of the prominent local businessman William Bartleman, is described as a lovely girl with blue eyes, dark brown hair, and fair skin. Seventeen-year-old Alexander wrote home: "You may rest assured that William has got a good wife, as everyone agrees who have known her... She comes of a respectable and sober Presbyterian family." William and Margaret moved in with Margaret's parents in the Bartleman home, two blocks from the river at 207 King Street.

By March of 1828, James's store in Washington was not doing well. Their brother Thomas in Kilmarnock was encouraging James to return home. James left his business in the care of his accountant Thomas Poincy, and traveled to New York to meet with a possible new partner. But after the meeting James decided against the new partnership. Instead, he boarded a ship there in New York, and returned to Scotland. James lived in

Kilmarnock along with his brother Thomas. He and a partner had a business in fabrics and silk.

Over the years James served as Councilman and Treasurer, and in the late 1840s as Magistrate of Kilmarnock. In 1854 James became Kilmarnock's first Registrar and took great pains to record several thousand birth dates of Kilmarnock residents from years earlier, including his family's.

James' niece Margaret, daughter of his sister Mary in Paterson, New Jersey, left the United States and went to Kilmarnock and cared for her Uncle James. James never married and lived in Kilmarnock for the rest of his life.

## William's Sister Travels

In the 1820s, America's weaving industry, centered in the northeast, could not produce the quality and quantity of fabrics and carpets that could be imported from Europe. Congress worked on protectionist taxes to encourage American weaving factories to catch up with British production. A firm in New York City named Andrews, Thompson, & Company had successfully imported carpets from Gregory, Thomson, & Company in Kilmarnock. Now they wanted to avoid the new import tariffs and produce their own carpets, but they needed people who had those technical skills. They saw the Scottish firm of Gregory, Thomson, & Company as their source for knowledge.

In Alexandria, William was well aware of the new taxes on imported carpets. He commented on it to his brother James, who had returned to Kilmarnock, writing that the taxes would make carpets too expensive to import.

While William was in America, the factory in Kilmarnock was expanding and changing with new technology. More weaving factories were opening and Kilmarnock produced and exported ever more carpets. New improved looms like the "Barrel Carpet Loom" produced more luxurious carpets made with three-ply yarns. One of the new factories was started by a younger member of the Thomson family, Robert Thomson, who opened a factory across town on his family's property on Nelson Street. The Thomson and the Gregory families had been close for generations, so it's not surprising that Robert married William's sister of two years younger, Mary.

Andrews, Thompson, & Company in New York City was run by Orrin Thompson, who was from Enfield, Connecticut. Enfield was a small town on the Connecticut River, where Freshwater Brook flows into the larger Connecticut River. In 1828 Orrin Thompson's company contracted with Gregory, Thomson, & Company in Kilmarnock to be supplied with hand-operated weaving looms and skilled workers from Kilmarnock. The site for his new company, which would later be named Thompsonville Carpet Manufacturing Company, would be in

Enfield. Orrin Thompson hired another firm to build a dam at Freshwater Brook to power the factory. The dam would be a big project and needed to be fourteen feet high and one hundred eighteen feet long.

The first group of twenty skilled weavers traveled from Kilmarnock in the summer of 1828, with a contract to work in Enfield, Connecticut for two years. Their passage was paid by the American company. Like William, the Kilmarnock weavers landed in New York City, without mishap or death from the journey. They were met in New York City and were escorted the one hundred forty miles north to Enfield.

On arriving in Enfield, the weavers were disappointed to find that there was no worker's housing, and there was no factory! They had to stay in three riverside taverns meant for boatmen. The dam in the river was also not completed, nor was the land cleared for factory construction. So instead of beginning their contracted work as expected, the men worked on finishing the dam, clearing the land, and building the factory. Months later, in the spring of 1829, the main factory building, White Mill, was complete. White Mill was a three-story, wood frame building with a bell tower, built over a mill stream that would power the factory. Foundations were being dug for tenement houses for workers.

The second group of workers to travel from Kilmarnock to the new factory in Connecticut later in 1829 included Robert Thomson and his wife Mary with their two young daughters. The other workers and their families also came from Robert Thomson's Kilmarnock factory. Robert was made superintendent at the new Thompsonville Carpet Manufacturing Company.

Those first two years in Connecticut were hard for Mary Thomson. Like her brother William, Mary was surprised at the extremely cold New England winters. She needed extra layers of clothing for her family, in a land where good fabric was hard to find. Mary wrote letters home to Kilmarnock asking for cloth, needles, and pins for sewing warm clothes. Mary also wrote that she missed green vegetables and oranges. Life in America was much more basic and much less civilized than in Great Britain.

Robert's management position at the Enfield factory did not go well. Robert found the "Yankees" to be "selfish, mean, and low" and that owner Orrin Thompson was the worst of them all. Everything Orrin Thompson said was law. There would be no chance for Robert to have a say in factory matters. Robert was used to being the boss, so this did not suit him well.

In the summer of 1830, William, now age 41, traveled from Alexandria with his family to visit his sister Mary and brother-in-law Robert in Connecticut. Later Mary commented on how supportive her older brother William was to her family.

After two years, in 1831 Mary and Robert Thomson left Thompsonville Carpet

Manufacturing in Enfield, Connecticut, and moved south to Paterson, New Jersey. They may have heard about Paterson, possibly from William, because it was known in the mid-1820s as the "Cotton Town of the U.S." Paterson is twenty-one miles northwest of New York City and has a great location on the Passaic River. Large waterfalls pour over massive, black rocks. Like in Scotland in the 1700s, and like in Enfield, Connecticut, this water was great for powering industry. There were a number of factories already on the banks of the Passaic River. Robert must have thought carefully about this decision to move, and saw great potential for his family. So they moved to Paterson with their two daughters and some of the Kilmarnock weavers. They had a third child, a boy who they called Tommy.

Mary Gregory Thomson, courtesy Karen Shaw

The Thomson's first years in Paterson in the early 1830s were economic boom years, which may have made starting a new weaving factory possible for Robert. But soon the bubble burst with the "Panic of 1837." Mary wrote about it to her brother James in Kilmarnock, saying that the factory and workers were struggling. Robert traveled to New York City but found it hard to sell his fabrics there. The recession lasted until the mid-1840s.

Mary and Robert Thomson lived not far from the factories, on Manchester Street. There was no school for girls in Paterson at that time, and Mary was interested in finding a good education for her girls. Like the rest of the Gregorys, Mary was especially interested in good music education. Unfortunately, though, the recession put a damper on those desires, and Mary wrote that private school in Elizabeth Town at $40 per quarter was too expensive for her family.

## William's Large Family

Although William didn't marry until 1822—fifteen years after arriving in America—he ultimately was married again in 1838 and raised a total of nine children. In 1824, William's first wife Margaret Bartleman gave birth to their first boy, Douglas. Lizzie came in 1826, and William in 1829. He had taken ownership of the McCrea dry goods business in 1827, and bought the property at 400-402 King Street across from today's City Hall. That same year there was a huge fire in Alexandria, which damaged William's building and dozens of others. By 1831,

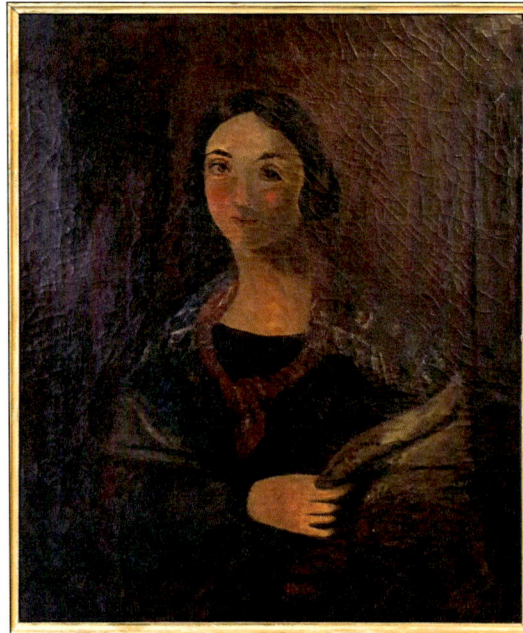

Mary D. Long, William's second wife. Courtesy Martica Gibson

William Gregory III, courtesy Gregory Gibson

he and Margaret were expecting their fourth child, who they would name Margaret.

Business was doing well, so William bought a twelve-year-old, two-story, brick tenant house at 329 North Washington Street for $4,000. This home at the corner of Princess Street was known as the Leadbeater house, as the Leadbeater family had been tenants. The house had a spacious side yard allowing ample room for the children to play. The lower part of the backyard had a brick-making kiln. Years later his children would play with the bricks left there. William now had experience with building, and he decided to raise the height of the building from two to four levels.

Two years after Maggie's birth, William's wife Margaret became ill with tuberculosis. In the hopes of restoring her health, William and Margaret set out on a sea voyage to the island of Barbados. On their trip, their ship came across heavy winds that blew them far out to sea towards Europe. They finally reached Bridgetown on Barbados on June 18, 1833. Margaret's health had not improved during this stressful journey, and she died the next day at the age of 33. The ship's captain however, would not take Margaret's body on board for the return trip because his sailors were superstitious. Eventually a merchant ship was found whose captain agreed to carry

The Gregory home on North Washington Street

Margaret's body, but only if it were in a lead coffin. Somehow, a lead coffin was found, and after a voyage of over a month via New York City, Margaret Bartleman Gregory was buried in the Presbyterian Cemetery in Alexandria. William was left to deal with his grief, and four young children to raise.

〜〜

In March of 1838 William remarried. At 2nd Presbyterian Church he married 29-year-old Mary Long. In 1842 William and Mary traveled to Kilmarnock, Scotland, with their baby daughter, Isobel, who they called Belle, to visit the Scottish family. Apparently, this was their last visit, as Mary always remembered it fondly. During their visit, the Gregorys traveled to the Highlands, leaving Belle in the care of Mary Mills, an orphaned young woman who was living with William's aunts in Kilmarnock.

On their return to America, the Gregorys brought Mary Mills with them to serve as nanny. The new Scottish nanny got along well with the Gregorys, and her services were much needed

# William Gregory III Family Tree

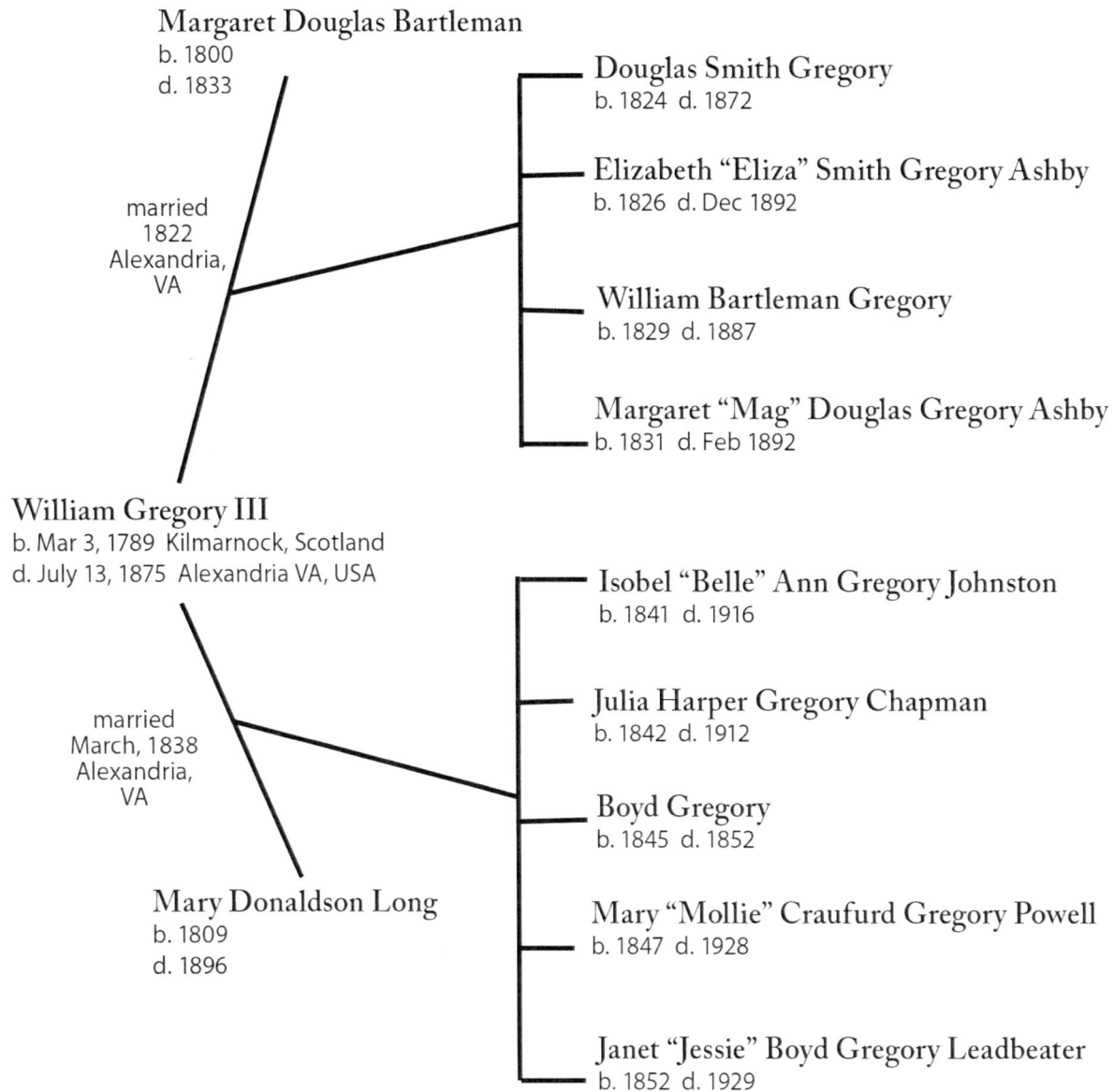

Margaret Douglas Bartleman
b. 1800
d. 1833

Douglas Smith Gregory
b. 1824 d. 1872

Elizabeth "Eliza" Smith Gregory Ashby
b. 1826 d. Dec 1892

William Bartleman Gregory
b. 1829 d. 1887

Margaret "Mag" Douglas Gregory Ashby
b. 1831 d. Feb 1892

married
1822
Alexandria,
VA

William Gregory III
b. Mar 3, 1789 Kilmarnock, Scotland
d. July 13, 1875 Alexandria VA, USA

Isobel "Belle" Ann Gregory Johnston
b. 1841 d. 1916

Julia Harper Gregory Chapman
b. 1842 d. 1912

Boyd Gregory
b. 1845 d. 1852

married
March, 1838
Alexandria,
VA

Mary Donaldson Long
b. 1809
d. 1896

Mary "Mollie" Craufurd Gregory Powell
b. 1847 d. 1928

Janet "Jessie" Boyd Gregory Leadbeater
b. 1852 d. 1929

in the following years. During the 1840s, three more Gregory children were born—a daughter named Julia, then a son, Boyd, and in 1847, Mary, who the family called Mollie. Fortunately the Gregory home on North Washington Street was spacious. It housed the four older children by Margaret, and Mary Gregory's growing family.

In 1849, William's third child, William Bartleman Gregory, was to travel to Edinburgh, Scotland, to study medicine. Before leaving for Scotland, young William walked three blocks to King Street to Mr. Grubb's studio, and had a sketch made of his little half-sister, two-year-old Mollie. A daguerreotype print was made which young William took with him to show the Gregory family in Kilmarnock, Scotland.

Mary "Mollie" Craufurd Gregory Powell, 1847-1928

The year 1852 brought both joy and grief to the Gregory household. Their youngest daughter Janet was born. In that same year, William and Mary's only son, 7-year-old Boyd, became ill with the flu, and died thereafter of meningitis. The family was devastated. By 1852, the Scottish nanny Mary Mills had worked for the Gregorys for almost ten years. She left the family to marry a man named William D'Arley. With four young daughters, Mary Gregory would need new help.

## Slaves

In the 1850s, America's first president, George Washington, had been gone for over fifty years. But due to the loss of their nanny Mary Mills in 1852, William Gregory III soon became indirectly connected to President George Washington's family via the purchase of slaves.

George Washington never had any children, but his wife Martha had four children from her former marriage to Daniel Parke Custis. Martha's grandson, named George Washington Parke Custis, was orphaned at the age of six, and adopted by George and Martha. They called him "Wash" and he grew up at Mount Vernon where he was spoiled by George and Martha. The President himself considered Wash to be incorrigible, lazy, and irresponsible. Wash attended university but never graduated. Why should he? He would be the heir to one of the largest fortunes in America. It was rumored that Wash took advantage of his position at Mount Vernon, and violated several of the enslaved women, fathering untold numbers of mulatto or mixed-race offspring.

One of the house slaves at Mount Vernon who was reputed to have suffered abuse by Wash was the most trusted servant in the household. Her name was Caroline Branham. When George Washington died in December of 1799, he and Martha were the owners of over three hundred enslaved people. Martha died in 1802, and at that point, Wash inherited many of the enslaved people from the Mount Vernon estate, including Caroline Branham, her children, and her enslaved husband, Peter Hardiman. Wash also inherited one thousand acres of land, which included a high hill that overlooked Washington City from the western side of the Potomac River. In addition to the Mount Vernon slaves, Wash also bought the people who had belonged to his mother. In all, Wash owned two hundred enslaved people.

In 1802, sixty-three of these slaves were brought to the inherited land, which was so large that it encompassed today's Fort Myer and Arlington National Cemetery. Although Caroline Branham must have been happy to have her family and husband with her on the farm, she was not allowed to enjoy it. Wash continued to commit rape with his subordinate servants. In 1806 he fathered a child with Caroline who was named Lucy, who is said to have resembled Wash's white daughter, Mary Custis.

At Wash's plantation, the enslaved people built their own log cabins for shelter. Over the next sixteen years and around the War of 1812, enslaved people built a mansion for Wash at the top of the hill, overlooking the city of Washington. The house was built in the style of a Greek temple, with enormous marble columns. It was called Arlington House, and today we know it as the Lee Mansion. Then, in 1852, Wash was aging. He didn't need the many enslaved people that he owned, but he may have preferred the money.

In 1852, William had lost his young son Boyd as well as his long-term childcare provider who had left to get married, and he had a new baby, Janet. William's eighth child, Mollie, later wrote a family history under her married name, Mary Gregory Powell, stating that in 1852 her father William purchased a family of five enslaved people from George Washington Parke Custis. Of the five enslaved people bought by William, a woman named Lucy Harrington and her infant son, Charles, were said to be freed. Other sources say Lucy Harrington was freed in 1846 by a Quaker merchant. Lucy's two daughters purchased by William, Eugenia and Sarah, were said to be granddaughters of Caroline Branham. They were mulatto or mixed race, ages 12 and 14. Mollie wrote that there was also a man named Walter who was apprenticed by William. The two enslaved servant girls did sewing, cleaning, waiting tables, and childcare.

William's wife Mary Gregory taught the enslaved girls to read and write. Eugenia would read

*Ali Baba and the Forty Thieves*, and told the story of Brer Rabbit and Tar Baby. By law the two girls were to be freed when they reached the age of 21.

## A New Cotton Factory

In 1846 William was part of a large project to build something that he knew a lot about: a cotton factory. William partnered with nine other men, including Robert Jamieson and William Stabler, to form the Mount Vernon Manufacturing Company, to make "textile products." An enormous, five-story brick building was constructed in 1847, two blocks north of William's house on North Washington Street. It was called the Mount Vernon Cotton Factory. Maybe William thought he might be part of cotton manufacturing once again, as his family was in Kilmarnock, Scotland.

The large building was built in the same style as the many cotton factories that still exist in many places in the Lowlands of Scotland. Like the Scottish factories, its walls were about four feet thick. The factory held one hundred twenty-four cotton fabric weaving looms and was powered by two steam engines. Machinery for the mill was bought from a factory about

The Cotton Factory at 515 North Washington Street is condos today.

thirty-three miles away in Laurel, Maryland. The cotton mill employed one hundred fifty people, mostly women, who worked eleven hours each day, earning from twelve to seventeen dollars per month.

The Mount Vernon Cotton Factory operated until the late 1850s. It had competition from manufacturing mills in New England. Today the building has been renovated into elegant apartments, the same as many of the factory buildings in Scotland.

## Prosperity in Alexandria

For nearly forty years after William's arrival in Alexandria, the city was not in Virginia. It was a part of Washington, D.C., which was across the Potomac River. That meant that Alexandrians could not vote for President, and had no representative in the nation's Congress. In the mid-1840s, there was no railroad in Alexandria, and the economy had been stagnant for years. When William wrote home that business was dull, he had good reason. In 1846 there was a growing desire to return the city to Virginia. The city petitioned Congress, and an act was passed to allow Alexandria to "retrocede" back to Virginia. In March of 1847, Alexandria became a part of Virginia once again. The city celebrated with a parade, and a speech by George Washington Parke Custis.

Following retrocession, the 1850s were a time of growth and prosperity for Alexandria. In 1851, a new tunnel was built for a rail line a few blocks south of King Street, called the Wilkes Street tunnel. This tunnel exists today and is used by people on foot and bicycle. This and other new rail lines helped the city to grow. Alexandria's population grew from approximately 9,000 to 13,000 people in the decade, and over five hundred homes were built.

Lives were transformed as new services suddenly became available. A new gas plant was built, and underground pipes were installed that provided lighting to streets and houses. Before the 1850s, homes in Alexandria had their own water wells, or people could use a public bath house for a small fee to bathe. In 1852, a new water reservoir was built on the south side of a hill at the western end of town called Shuter's Hill. Pipes were laid, and water flowed to the Gregory home for the first time in June of 1852. Later on in the 1960s, some of the residential water wells were excavated by archaeologists.

After the death of William's son Boyd and the birth of his daughter Janet in 1852, things changed in the Gregory house on North Washington Street. His son William Bartleman was away in Scotland, studying medicine. The three other older children left home to start their own lives. Mollie Gregory was a young child, and was being cared for by her enslaved nannies, Sarah and Eugenia.

Years later, Mollie wrote in her family history about a parade that took place along Cameron

Street, which was the town's main street at the time. Cameron Street stopped at North Washington Street, two blocks from the Gregory house, so Mollie, Eugenia, and the others walked over to see the parade. At the corner of North Washington and Cameron Streets, they watched the mayor, town dignitaries, and Alexandria's fire companies parade up Cameron to Christ Church, turn right and left up towards the Court House on Columbus Street. They saw Alexandria's "Friendship Fire Engine," acquired in 1851, which remains on display today in the Friendship Firehouse Museum. Mollie wrote, "The procession wound up Cameron St. to Columbus to the Court House where George Washington Parke Custis was to read the "Farewell Address" of Washington to his army at Annapolis."

The Court House was in the 300 block of Columbus Street, across from today's Kate Waller Barrett Branch Library. Mollie wrote that the parade ended with a company of about twenty men, including her father William, who were being celebrated as the "Old Defenders of 1812"— surviving veterans of the War of 1812. William was in his sixties.

In the summertime, the Gregory children would walk the six blocks down to the Potomac River, to "Old Point," which may refer to the original "West's Point," where Alexandria's first wharf had been built in the mid-1700s. From the Gregory's windows, Mollie could see cows grazing by what she called the "Rectory," which may have been the house of the clergy for Christ Church.

## Freedom From Slavery

The Gregory's enslaved nannies—Eugenia and Sarah—were freed around 1859 and 1861, at the ages of 21, in accordance with the law. Mollie writes that Sarah married a "good but delicate" man named John Crier. They had one daughter, but John died young of tuberculosis. Eugenia married a man named Rudolf Popham Thompson. Molly felt it was of interest to comment on the skin tone of each man, saying that John Crier was "darker than Sarah" and that Rudolf Thompson was "nearly white." Rudolf was a barrel maker and roofer by trade. He and Eugenia had eight children who all became barbers later in life, except one who became a teacher. Eugenia kept a successful "Market Garden" in the northwestern section of Alexandria on a property called "Colross," which filled one city block at 1100 Oronoco Street, today part of the Parker Gray Historic District. In 1930 the historic Colross house was dismantled and moved to Princeton, New Jersey. Eugenia died in 1897.

## Country Home

William retired from the dry goods business in the early 1850s when he was in his sixties. With Alexandria's booming economy, coal-powered steam trains were bringing wheat into the city from the Virginia countryside. It would make sense to process the wheat into flour in Alexandria. A large flour mill was built along the Potomac River, south of King Street, called Pioneer Mill. This mill, along with Smith & Perkins locomotive works which made steam engines, Smoot's tannery, Green's furniture factory, and the Mount Vernon Cotton Factory, were all less than a mile from the Gregory's house. The air quality in Alexandria must have been poor. Mollie came down with an extended case of whooping cough, which couldn't be cured.

William decided to find a healthier place for his family, and began looking for a house in the country to buy. He found a farm outside of Alexandria, about five miles out Little River Turnpike in Fairfax County, on a hill overlooking a stream called Holmes Run. William named his new summer home "Strathblane" after his ancestral home in Stirlingshire, Scotland—a village about ten miles north of Glasgow. William did renovations to the house, built outbuildings, and planted trees. At the base of the hill, down by the stream, were enormous cherry trees. The horse-drawn carriages used to carry the family to the farm would be parked at the bottom of the hill under the large, shady cherry trees. The family would spend their summers at Strathblane and return to Alexandria in November for the beginning of school.

## Slavery and War in the 1860s

By the late 1850s, the issue of slavery was coming to a head. An abolitionist named John Brown lead a revolt against slavery in a town seventy miles northwest of Alexandria called Harper's Ferry. All of the northern states plus California had abolished slavery. Alexandria was a southern town, positioned firmly in the pro-slavery camp. It had the nation's largest slave dealers less than one mile from William's house. At 1315 Duke Street, a slave operation had opened in 1828 by two men named Franklin and Armfield. Enslaved people were auctioned at Alexandria's waterfront, or were marched to the small basement prison on Duke Street where they were shackled to the wall, or held in an outdoor pen until it was their time to be shipped or marched in shackles to southern plantations. In 1858 the slave operation was bought and continued to be run by Price, Birch, and Company.

The presidential election of 1860 brought Abraham Lincoln into the White House. His Republican party was committed to the "ultimate extinction" of slavery. This lead to southern states deciding to flee the Union of American states. Virginia voted to remove itself from the Union in May of 1861. On May 23, Alexandrians voted to secede from the Union as well. Alexandria, being across the river from the nation's capital, Washington, D.C., did not remain in this new southern confederacy for long.

Civil War arrived in Alexandria the very next day when Union troops arrived. Soldiers marched across the Long Bridge from Washington and entered Alexandria on North

Washington Street, passing William's house. William's children were dressed by their new nanny and hurried out to watch the passing soldiers. Brightly dressed troops called the New York Zouaves arrived at the foot of Cameron Street on three steamships, guarded by a ship called USS Pawnee.

All of the Gregory men eventually signed the Oath of Allegiance to the Federal government. The Gregory's sympathies however, were with the Confederacy, the southern states. William believed that the skirmish would be over in a few weeks. But by 1862 some of the family's young men were serving in the Confederate Army. William's younger daughters traveled with their older sisters and their families to Culpeper, Virginia. They may have ridden the Orange and Alexandria Railroad seventy miles southwest to Culpeper Courthouse, where Confederate troops were training.

William's son, William Bartleman, age 33, was now a doctor. He went to the front lines and treated wounded confederate soldiers. The Union army captured him and brought him to Alexandria's war prison, the cotton mill building that his father had helped build. On the way to jail, they passed his family home, two blocks away, and he asked if he could stop in and greet his family. This was allowed. His mother was home and took his uniform in exchange for new clothes and a coat. While in the cotton factory jail two blocks from home, William Bartleman was able to see his young sister Janet (Jessie) who would call to him through a knot hole in the fence. His captors made sure he signed the Oath of Allegiance to the U.S. government.

## Samuel Morse: A Pro-Slavery Voice

In the 1830s and 1840s, the single-wire telegraph machine was being invented by an artist and inventor from Massachusetts named Samuel Morse, who developed Morse code. Morse was almost the same age as William. Although the North was anti-slavery, Morse was one northern voice vehemently supporting slavery. He was known nationally for his articles declaring slavery to be "protection and judicious guidance" to a "barbarous race." William, who was a slave owner in the South, read Morse's articles in the Alexandria newspaper. He may have felt the need to defend his slaveholder status to his family, because in March of 1863 he wrote to his sister Susan, saying that he forwarded an article to their brother about this issue:

> I sent John a newspaper today, containing Professor Morse's views of Lincoln's proclamation of freedom to the Blacks etc. etc. Dr. Morse is a wise & good man and very many such among us hold these opinions. It is an article that should be read by all who take an interest in the slavery question and are governed, not by their judgements, but by their feelings.

# Effects of the Civil War

Most of William's letter of March 22, 1863 to Susan in Kilmarnock did not discuss slavery, but rather other concerns of the day, including childhood memories, wartime Alexandria, and whether he might ever see his home again. The photo he mentioned is held in the Special Collections at Alexandria's Kate Waller Barrett Branch Library:

March 22, 1863

Dear Susan,

We are all much gratified by the receipt of a letter from our niece, Margaret Thomson, enclosing your photographic likeness - I have no doubt but that it is good in resemblance as it certainly is in execution and I prize it very highly as being that of the only living person associated with my earliest recollections.

I have a distinct remembrance of the Strand Foot House and all its rooms - our Mother's chamber where we locked ourselves in once, and could not open it again, and how much frightened we were, especially, when we saw Father placing a ladder against the wall and entering the window even then took under the bed expecting a payment but were happy to be relieved by his kind voice, offering us that we were not to be punished. I remember where the "Chest of Drawers" stood where we put our spelling books on our return from school.

I also remember Father taking us to school when there was a great speat in the water. I remember Mall Hodge who died about that time. Also an indistinct recollection of a brother of hers, who when catching small fish in a basket, when the water was very high, was dragged into the rapid current and perished. I believe that we used to come in for a share of his catchings.

My memory is well charged with little circumstances that occurred before we left Strand Foot. We were frequent visitors at old Dr. Morris's, old Mrs. Darby, Boyd Miller's mother, Mrs. Henderson's, auld Ms. Bobby Morris next door to us. Jean Aitken etc. etc.

I had a letter from our sister Mary a few months ago. She remarked we were now a very aged family and with little prospect of our meeting on earth again. Unless I was to visit them. This I may do if life and health is spared. But I indulge in no hope of ever revisiting my native land. My affairs are a good deal deranged. My family scattered and dispersed and I suppose some of them suffering without my having it in my power to help them as I would wish. I sent them over $100 in bank notes a few weeks ago, which I believe reached them as the bearer of them got through the Armies.

William's older sister Susan Gregory. Photo sent to him in Alexandria, from his niece Margaret Thomson. This photo is in the Special Collections at Alexandria's Kate Waller Barrett Branch Library.

Our city is very quiet and good order kept by the Military. We have a good many Regiments in the neighborhood, but the soldiers are not allowed to come in unless with a pass. The Provost Marshall at present will give no man one unless he took the Oath of Allegiance, even to go outside of town. Douglas formerly had a pass—for himself and family, for the month. Now he gets a weekly pass and only for himself.

You may imagine that I am very sick of things. We have suffered greatly in Alexandria, but other places near Fredericksburg, Winchester, etc still more. We have reason to be thankful that we have good houses to live in and the greatest abundance of provisions at Baltimore rates. As tho they are high—Tea, coffee, sugar are just about double they were 12 months ago. Dry goods, both cotton and woollen are much upwards of double in the Southern Confederacy, the prices not of luxuries alone but of the most common necessaries increased to an almost fabulous rate.

During the Civil War, Union troops took over William's summer house, Strathblane. Trees were chopped down, furniture was destroyed, and soldiers carved their initials in the woodwork. Finally, in November of 1865, the Civil War came to an end. After the war William returned to his country home, Strathblane, and refurbished it. The Gregory family spent many a summer enjoying the property in a very rural Fairfax County.

Nearly a century later, in the early 1950s, Alexandria expanded into Fairfax County by annexing a large amount of land and doubling the size of the city. Strathblane became part of Alexandria's West End as city streets, housing, and shopping malls were built up.

# An End

In July of 1875, after living all of his adult life in Alexandria, William Gregory III died of a heart attack. Mollie wrote to her Uncle James in Kilmarnock:

> My dear Uncle,
> You have heard of our dear Father's sudden death. For some time past he has been subject to attacks of pain in his chest and the region of the heart. On that day he had one at about 7 o'clock by his changing his coat and throwing it from him. He took some ether and said to Mother, "I will lie down" and walked to the bed. Brother William sent for Doctor Lewis who arrived shortly and ordered mustard plasters to his feet which were becoming cold. The family were all sent for, but he was gone just as sister Margaret and Julia entered the room.
>
> The last day of his life he seemed quite happy. He signed a deed and wrote 2 business letters. After dinner, Jessie and Mary played for him some Scotch tunes, "Niel Gow's Lamentation for Abercairnie" and "Blue Bells of Scotland." … His death is a great blow to us all & seems but the commencement of the breaking up of a happy family.
>
> The whole community unite in their sympathy with us & although many people are out of town, It was the largest funeral I ever saw. Very many colored people were present, walking to the Graveyard behind the carriages. Mr. Dinwiddie's remarks were beautiful. He referred to the time when Father left Greenock. How he went into his cabin and fell upon his knees, seeking the protection of Heaven upon his venture into the New World. … The twilight deepens into night, so I will close as I can hardly see the lines.
> Your loving niece, Mary C. Gregory

The Gregory family continued to live at 329 North Washington Street until 1937, when the house was sold.

Of William's ten brothers and sisters from Kilmarnock, four came to live in America. Peter died in Alexandria shortly after arriving. Alexander wrote of an interest in leaving Alexandria and moving to South Carolina or Georgia. William sent him to New York City for long spells, to monitor incoming goods. He died in 1835, at age 32. James returned to Kilmarnock and lived at 3 Nelson Street, which is now a vacant lot. William's sister Mary and her husband Robert Thomson stayed in Paterson, New Jersey, where she died at the age of 90.

In Kilmarnock, carpet manufacturers existed throughout the 1800s. There were from five to eight companies at any given time. Gregory, Thomson, and Company operated at 24 Green Street in the center of Kilmarnock until about 1903 when there were three weaving companies left. Green Street is the same street that runs parallel to Kilmarnock Water. Up by the bridge it is still called High Street, even though town center has always been at the "Cross"—the big intersection with the Rabbie Burns and John Wilson statue. Spinning and carpet manufacture continued until the 1960s in Kilmarnock, when most factories closed. The church where the Gregory family worshiped is now a funeral parlor, but the graveyard next to it still exists. Several Gregory family gravestones are located next to the building's back entrance.

# Final Thoughts

People often refer to the vast difference in the length of human history in Europe compared to America's short existence. However, the birth of modern cities on both sides of the Atlantic actually happened at about the same time. Scotland entered its massive economic and building expansion in the mid-1700s due to imports of cotton from the new world. The settling of America fueled the growth of Scotland. Land on both sides was seen as a wilderness that needed to be molded to support human needs. In Scotland the Clyde River went through a massive dredging and deepening in the late 1700s so ships could sail into Glasgow.

On the other side in America, the James River was dredged to allow ships access to ports closer to the city of Richmond, Virginia. The Cape Fear River in Wilmington, North Carolina was a major port. Today's shallow Hunting Creek in Alexandria was deep enough that ships sailed inland to reach the Cameron Mills. As Alexandria was growing, so was Kilmarnock, Greenock, and Glasgow in Scotland. In Virginia old forests with massive trees were seen as getting in the way of farming, and were removed. Scotland didn't have the trees necessary for its housing expansion, so ships sailed from the Clyde River to bring back timber from Canada. Posts can still be seen sticking up in the Clyde River today, where logs were stored so the wood was preserved until its use by builders.

No one knows exactly how many Scots left their country. Experts estimate that the number

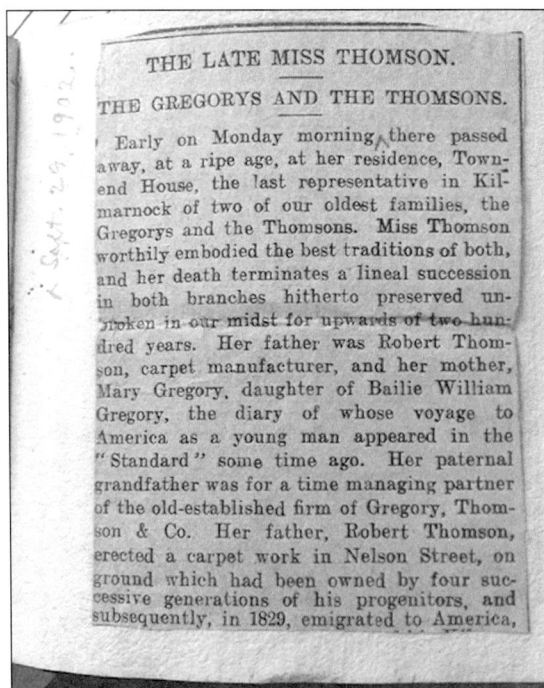

Newspaper article in Kilmarnock from September 29, 1902

## THE LATE MISS THOMSON.

### THE GREGORYS AND THE THOMSONS.

Early on Monday morning, there passed away, at a ripe age, at her residence, Town-end House, the last representative in Kilmarnock of two of our oldest families, the Gregorys and the Thomsons. Miss Thomson worthily embodied the best traditions of both, and her death terminates a lineal succession in both branches hitherto preserved unbroken in our midst for upwards of two hundred years. Her father was Robert Thomson, carpet manufacturer, and her mother, Mary Gregory, daughter of Bailie William Gregory, the diary of whose voyage to America as a young man appeared in the "Standard" some time ago. Her paternal grandfather was for a time managing partner of the old-established firm of Gregory, Thomson & Co. Her father, Robert Thomson, erected a carpet work in Nelson Street, on ground which had been owned by four successive generations of his progenitors, and subsequently, in 1829, emigrated to America,

William Gregory III's grave marker at the Gregory family grave site, Presbyterian Cemetery in Alexandria, Virginia

is in the millions over several hundred years. Scots were one of the first groups to immigrate to America in large numbers. They had many fellow countrymen in America at the time. Scottish cooking, religion and speech were normal. People spoke English and many went to the Presbyterian Church. People ate biscuits and pies and meat with gravy. But as people from all over the world arrived in America, our ancestors changed. Hot summers made us love the outdoors. Fierce, bright winters made us bundle up. We ate new and different vegetables. We discovered spice. The words that rolled off our tongues took on a different tone. After just a few generations, many people have lost touch with their Scottish roots.

Scotland went through massive changes in the 1700s. Scottish cities grew with workers arriving to work in the new textile industry. Growth was powered by water wheels on rivers, and growth was fueled by cheap cotton coming from America. There was a population explosion, requiring the building of towns in Scotland. But for many people, new opportunities in Scotland could not rival the lure of financial freedom in the budding country of the United States.

People trickled out of Scotland one by one. They flowed out of Scottish harbors family by family. They spent all their money on the journey. They disposed of generations of belongings and took the risk of ten long weeks at sea, to try their luck at a new life in an unforgiving land.

There may be two ways to see Scottish migration to America. Was migration caused by abhorrent, greedy behavior by British lords and landowners and their self-interest, abuse of power, and denigration of people? Or was migration caused by this new money-based economy and people's hope for a better quality of life and new opportunities? Possibly, both may be true.

# Bibliography

Aitchison, Peter and Andrew Cassell. *The Lowland Clearances, Scotland's Silent Revolution 1760–1830.* Birlinn, Edinburgh, Scotland, 2003.

Alexander, Derek and Gordon McCrae. *Renfrewshire, A Scottish County's Hidden Past.* Birlinn, Edinburgh, Scotland, 2012.

Cameron, Viola Root. *Emigrants from Scotland to America 1774–1775: Copied from a Loose Bundle of Treasury Papers in the Public Records Office, London, England.* Clearfield Company, Baltimore, MD, 1976.

Campsie, Alison. *Steel Industry in Scotland: A Short History.* The Scotsman, Sept, 2016.

Davidson, James D.G. *Scots and the Sea: A Nation's Lifeblood.* Mainstream Publishing Co., Edinburgh, 2003.

Dobson, David. *The Original Scots Colonists of Early America 1612–1783.* Genealogical Publishing Co., Baltimore, MD, 1989.

Dobson, David. *Ships from Scotland to America 1628–1828.* Genealogical Publishing Co., Baltimore, MD, 1998.

Dunbar, Erica Armstrong. *Never Caught: The Washingtons' Relentless Pursuit of Their Runaway Slave, Ona Judge.* Simon & Schuster, 37 Ink, New York, NY, 2017.

Graham, Barbara. *Kilmarnock Carpet Weavers in America.* Kilmarnock District History Group Newsletter, No. 42, Burns Monument Centre, Kilmarnock, Scotland, September, 1980.

Gregory, William, Peter Gregory, James Gregory, Mary Gregory Thomson, Grace Powell, and Edith Snowden. Letters Written 1807–1978.

Johnson, Samuel and James Boswell. *A Journey to the Western Islands of Scotland and The Journal of a Tour to the Hebrides.* Penguin Books, London, England, 1775.

Latimer, John. *1812 War with America.* Belknap Press, Harvard University, Cambridge, MA, 2007.

Lee, Antoinette J., ed; Mrs. Hugh B. Cox, comp. HARC, Feb. 1968. *William Gregory Building, 400–402 King Street, Alexandria, Virginia, Photographs, Written Historical and Descriptive Data,* Historic American Buildings Survey, Office of Archaeology and Historic Preservation, Nov. 1975.

Leepson, Marc. *The First Union Civil War Martyr: Elmer Ellsworth, Alexandria, and the American Flag.* The Alexandria Chronical, A publication of the Alexandria Historical Society, Fall 2011.

Leyburn, James G. *The Scotch-Irish: A Social History.* The University of North Carolina Press, Durham, NC, 1962.

Mallamo, Lance. *A Dyed-in-the-Wool Alexandrian.* Alexandria Times, Out of the Attic, Feb. 2, 2017.

Mallamo, Lance. *A Historic Property with a Bright Future.* Alexandria Times, Out of the Attic, Jan. 8, 2015.

Mallamo, Lance and Amy Bertsch. *The Expansion West and Its Impact on Street Names.* Alexandria Times, Out of the Attic, Sept. 8, 2016.

Meyer, Duane. *The Highland Scots of North Carolina 1732–1776.* University of North Carolina Press, Chapel Hill, NC, 1966.

Miller, T. Michael, comp. *Artisans and Merchants of Alexandria, Virginia 1780–1820.* Volume I and II, Alexandria Library, Lloyd House, Heritage Books, 1991, 1992.

Miller, T. Michael. *Portrait of a Town, Alexandria, District of Columbia (Virginia) 1820–1830.* Heritage Books, Berwyn Heights, MD, 1995.

Nelson, Kay Shaw. *The Art of Scottish-American Cooking.* Pelican Publishing Co., New Orleans, LA, 2007.

Pope, Michael Lee. *Hidden History of Alexandria, DC.* The History Press, Charleston, SC, 2011.

Powell, Mary Gregory. *Reminiscences of Our Childhood.* (undated).

Powell, Mary Gregory. *The History of Old Alexandria, Virginia.* 1928.

Powell, Mary Gregory, Introduction by T. Michael Miller. *Scenes of Childhood.* The Fireside Sentinel, The Alexandria Library, Lloyd House Newsletter, January, 1990.

Smith, William Francis and T. Michael Miller. *A Seaport Saga: Portrait of Old Alexandria, Virginia.* The Donning Company Publishers, Virginia Beach, VA, 1989.

Swain, Emily, Paul P. Kreisa, Jacqueline M. McDowell, Geri Knight-Iska, and Nancy Powell. *Assessment and Intensive Archaeological Investigation for 513–515 N. Washington St, Alexandria, VA.* March, 25, 2016.

*The Alexandria Post Office: A History of More Than Stamps.* Alexandria Times, Out of the Attic, Jan. 20, 2019.

# Websites

BBC News *Scotland's Forgotten Clearances.* Scotland, UK, May 16, 2003 <http://news.bbc.co.uk/2/hi/uk_news/scotland/3030889.stm>

City of Alexandria *Alexandria and the War of 1812* <www.alexandriava.gov/1812>

Cunningham, Sean *The Secret History of George Washington's Slave Descendants.* InsideHook, October 29, 2016 <https://www.insidehook.com/article/history/the-secret-history-of-george-washingtons-slave-descendants>

Dalmadan *Colour on the Clyde.* <www.dalmadan.com>

Donaldson, Susan <https://auldearlston.blogspot.com/>

Gillen, Vincent *Shipbuilding in Inverclyde.* Cartsburn Publishing, Inverclyde, Scotland, 2017 <https://www.inverclydeshipbuilding.com/shipbuilding-in-inverclyde>

Gregory, William *William Gregory's Journal, From Fredericksburg, VA, to Philadelphia, PA, 30th of September, 1765, to 16th October, 1765.* The William and Mary Quarterly, Volume 13, Omohundro Institute of Early American History and Culture, 1905, JSTOR <https://archive.org/details/jstor-1916147>

Findlay, C. Scottish Steelworks History *History of the Iron and Steel Industry in Scotland: In Relation to Clydebridge and Clyde Iron.* <https://cfindlay17.wixsite.com/clydebridge/history-of-iron-and-steel-in-scotla>

Loney, John *Jules Verne.* <https://irvinehistorynotes.yolasite.com/jules-verne.php>

MacLeod, Jessie, Associate Curator, *Caroline Branham.* George Washington's Mount Vernon <mountvernon.org/library/digitalhistory/digital-encyclopedia/article/caroline-branham>

Marshall, Seth *The War of 1812 & The U.S. Navy.* The Military Historian, January 4, 2015 <https://military-historian.squarespace.com/blog/2015/1/4/the-war-of-1812-the-us-navy>

National Museum of American History, Behring Center *On the Water: Stories form Maritime America*, <https://americanhistory.si.edu/on-the-water>

National Park Service *The fall of Fort Washington and the Battle of White House Landing.* <https://www.nps.gov/fowa/learn/historyculture/the-fall-of-fort-washington-and-the-battle-of-white-house-landing.htm>

Old Roads of Scotland *Roads and Tracks of Ayrshire.* <oldroadsofscotland.com/coaches.htm>

Prom, William J. *The U.S. Navy in the War of 1812: Winning the Battle, Losing the War.*

The Maritime Executive, March 24, 2021 <https://maritime-executive.com/editorials/the-u-s-navy-in-the-war-of-1812-winning-the-battle-losing-the-war>

Reschke, Dino *William Gregory III*. Immigrant Alexandria: A UMW History Project <http://immigrantalexandria.org/blog/william-gregory-iii/>

Roberts, Jay *Candidates for a Historical Marker: Robert T. Hooe.* Jaybird's Jottings, Alexandria, VA, March 3, 2016 <https://jay.typepad.com/william_jay/2016/03/candidates-for-a-historical-marker-robert-t-hooe.html>

The Waterloo Directory of English Newspapers and Periodicals 1800-1900, NC State University Libraries, Raleigh, NC <https://www.lib.ncsu.edu/databases/waterloo-directory-english-newspapers-and-periodicals-1800-1900>

Virginia Places *Ports in Virginia.* <www.virginiaplaces.org/transportation/shiptransport.html>

Wikipedia. *Renfrewshire.* <https://en.wikipedia.org/wiki/Renfrewshire>

Wikipedia. *History of Glasgow.* <https://en.wikipedia.org/wiki/History_of_Glasgow>

# About the Author

Ellen Hamilton was born in Durham, North Carolina, where her grandfather taught English at Duke University, and her grandmother was an aspiring writer. The family moved to Pittsburgh, Pennsylvania in the early 1970s where Ellen's father taught English Literature at the University of Pittsburgh. In the late 1970s and early '80s, the family lived in Kassel, Germany, where Ellen's father taught American History at a new German university. Ellen attended German schools where she was immersed in the German language, and also studied French and Spanish. After high school, Ellen worked as an au pair in France and a street musician in Spain. She returned to the U.S. to study Fine Art and Printmaking at Virginia Commonwealth University in Richmond, Virginia. She moved to Alexandria in 1992, and returned to higher education to study Communication Design at Northern Virginia Community College. She worked as an in-house graphic designer at Thompson Publishing Group in Washington, D.C., and in 2007 she opened her own in-house design studio in Alexandria. After finding a stone tool made by Native Americans while digging in her back yard, Ellen became interested in archaeology. She served on the Alexandria Archaeological Commission for six years, where she learned about Alexandria's history. In 2001 Ellen married a Scot from near Glasgow, Scotland. After visiting that Lowland region a number of times, she was given a book about Scotland's history. She became aware of her own Scottish roots, and decided to make a film to tell the story of migration from Scotland to the United States. After many years of research and writing, she wrote the story with the result being this book.